CONTENTS

D0186909

List of Illustrations

PREFACE

With many artists – and not only those of earlier time – we must feel that we know far too little of their lives, their personalities, and their attitude towards their painting and their age. But with Constable the problem is that there is almost too much information about all these aspects and that we are in danger of being swamped by the detail. His correspondence with his friends, comment, criticism, and personal anecdote have been preserved to a remarkable degree; and considering how much is usually lost sight of in the course of a century an outstanding proportion not only of his ambitious pictures but also of his preparatory studies have been traced and recorded.

In the present book I have attempted to survey and compress the range of our knowledge in its existing state, and to concentrate upon the points which seem to me to require most emphasis for an understanding of the man and his work. Accordingly, while I have dealt somewhat summarily with the facts of his life, I have given rather more attention than usual to the ground in which his painting was based and out of which it sprung. I have also, in counterbalance to the prevailing tendency to award primacy of consideration to the oil sketches, stressed the importance of the six great paintings of the Stour – the canal scenes – into which Constable put his most intense intellectual labour, and on which he staked his own claim to the regard of posterity. The choice of illustrations has been made to reflect this balance of interests.

I am indebted generally to all the pioneers of Constable scholarship, to Leslie, Holmes, Shirley, Kay. Their publications are listed in the Bibliography, but, to present a text uninterrupted with footnotes, I have only provided a minimum of references to these and the other authorities I have consulted. I must here record my particular and overriding debt to Mr R. B. Beckett's monumental 'Correspondence and other Memorials of John Constable, R.A.' Unfortunately only a portion of this has yet been printed, but the complete typescript which he has generously deposited in the Library of the Victoria and Albert Museum for the free use of all scholars is an indispensable source of Constable studies and a truly remarkable achievement. One personal indebtedness which cannot as yet be linked with a printed source is the insight I have derived by talking with, and reading the theses of, two young American scholars who are breaking entirely fresh ground in Constable studies, Mr Louis Hawes and Mr Charles Rhyne.

GRAHAM REYNOLDS

BIOGRAPHICAL SUMMARY

1776 John Constable was born in East Bergholt, Suffolk,
on 11 June, the second son of Golding Constable, a
well-to-do mill-owner, and Ann Watts. His early
fondness for painting was encouraged by his friendship with John Dunthorne, a plumber and glazier
of East Bergholt, who was an amateur painter.
Others who encouraged him were Sir George Beaumont and Dr Fisher, later Bishop of Salisbury.

1796 Met J. T. ('Antiquity') Smith at Edmonton and made
drawings of picturesque cottages under his influence.

1799 Came to London in February with a letter of introduction to Joseph Farington, resolved to become a
professional painter. Entered the Royal Academy
Schools as a probationer in March.

1800 Enrolled as a student of the Royal Academy Schools
on 19 February. His curriculum included studies
from the antique, the nude model, and anatomical
drawings. In the summer he stayed by himself
sketching in Helmingham Park, the grounds of a
seat of Lord Dysart.

1801 Painted for Mr John Reade the view of *Old Hall,
East Bergholt*, his first considerable commission.
Went on a sketching tour of the Peak District,
Derbyshire, in August.

1802 Exhibited for the first time at the Royal Academy,
his entry being an unidentified 'Landscape'. Visited
Windsor in May and was at East Bergholt in the
summer and autumn. It was in this year that he de-
clared in his letter to John Dunthorne his intention of

becoming 'a natural painter'. He bought a studio in East Bergholt, near his parents' house.

1803 Exhibited four landscapes at the Royal Academy. In April made the trip from London to Deal in the East Indiaman *Coutts*, making many drawings of shipping, influenced by Van de Velde. Then he went to East Bergholt for the summer.

1804 Constable did not exhibit this year; according to Farington, he spent much of his time at East Bergholt painting portraits of the local farmers and their wives; he also visited Hampshire. First saw 'The Château de Steen' by Rubens in Sir George Beaumont's collection in 1804.

1805 Exhibited one landscape at the Royal Academy; was commissioned to paint the altarpiece for Brantham Church, *Christ blessing the Children*.

1806 A water-colour of the Battle of Trafalgar was his only exhibit at the Royal Academy in 1806. In June he was at East Bergholt, and later at Epsom. In the autumn paid a visit of some two months to the Lake District and made many studies of mountain scenery. Whilst the water-colours are in the style of Girtin the sketches in oil show the first signs of Constable's mature brilliance and naturalism; he began to make records of the weather on these drawings.

1807 Spent most of this year in London, and copied a portrait by Reynolds for Lord Dysart. His three exhibits at the Royal Academy were of Lake District scenes.

1808 Again exhibited three Lake District scenes at the Royal Academy, and visited East Bergholt in the summer.

1809 Visited Epsom again, and there and in East Bergholt made some sketches which reveal the progress of his style towards freedom of expression. He also stayed with Mr Henry Greswold Lewis at Malvern Hall. On his autumn visit to East Bergholt met Maria Bicknell and fell in love with her.

1810 Exhibited two pictures entitled *A Landscape* and *A Churchyard* (in the Tate Gallery) at the Royal Academy in 1810, and painted his second altarpiece, *Christ blessing the Bread and Wine*, for Nayland Church.

1811 In this year Constable's exhibits at the Royal Academy comprised *Twilight* and *Dedham Vale: Morning*. Visited Suffolk in the spring and paid his first visit to Salisbury in the autumn; this was probably the occasion of his first meeting with John Fisher, who was to become his closest friend. His attachment to Maria Bicknell became known during this year, and he received her father's permission to write to her in October, but the engagement was protracted owing to the opposition of Maria's grandfather, Dr Rhudde, rector of East Bergholt.

1812 His exhibits at the Royal Academy were *Salisbury: Morning* (in the Louvre), a view of Flatford Mill, and two small landscapes. Spent most of the summer in Suffolk, and his open-air sketching reveals the renewed influence of Rubens.

1813 Exhibited at the Royal Academy *Landscape: Boys Fishing* and a second landscape. Spent most of the summer and autumn in Suffolk, filling a remarkable small sketch-book with drawings of the countryside, between July and October.

1814 Exhibited at the Royal Academy *Landscape:*

Ploughing scene in Suffolk, also *Landscape: the ferry*. Visited Feering and southern Essex in June and spent much of the rest of the year in Suffolk, filling another small sketch-book, in which he made many preparatory designs for *Stour Valley and Dedham Village*.

1815   Five paintings and three drawings exhibited at the Royal Academy, including *Boatbuilding near Flatford Mill*, which he had painted in the open air. His mother died early this year and he was in Suffolk in May. Left London again for Suffolk on 6 July, and remained there most of the year, being detained during December by his father's serious illness.

1816   Exhibited *The Wheatfield* and *A Wood: Autumn* at the Royal Academy. His father died on 14 May. Spent some of the summer in Suffolk and paid two visits to Wivenhoe. The long engagement which had harassed his nerves over the last five years was now over; he was married by his friend John Fisher to Maria Bicknell on 2 October at St Martin-in-the-Fields, and they spent part of the honeymoon staying with Fisher at his vicarage at Osmington, Dorsetshire. On this visit Constable sketched Netley Abbey and the environs of Weymouth Bay.

1817   Exhibited four works at the Royal Academy: *Flatford Mill on the River Stour*; *A Cottage*; *Wivenhoe Park, Essex, the seat of Major-General Rebow*, and a portrait of John Fisher, still in the Fisher family collection. Spent ten weeks of the summer at East Bergholt. His first child, John Charles, was born on 4 December.

1818   Exhibited at the Royal Academy four landscapes and two drawings, one of the latter being entitled

Elms. He did a certain amount of sketching in the Home Counties, including Windsor.

1819   The first of his six-foot canal scenes *The White Horse*, exhibited at the Royal Academy; it was bought by John Fisher. His second child, Maria Louisa (Minna), was born on 19 July. He took a house at Hampstead for the first time at the end of the summer, and from now on scenes of that district figure largely in his work. Elected A.R.A. on 1 November.

1820   Second large canal scene, *Stratford Mill*, exhibited at the Royal Academy, together with *A View of Harwich Lighthouse*. Stayed with Fisher at Salisbury in July and August, settled his wife and children at Hampstead, and paid a brief visit to Malvern Hall.

1821   The chief of Constable's four exhibits was his third large canal scene, *The Hay Wain*. His third child, Charles Golding Constable, was born on 29 March. Accompanied Archdeacon John Fisher on his visitation of Berkshire in June and paid a visit to Fisher at Salisbury in November. It was in this year that he began his systematic study of 'skying'.

1822   Exhibits at the Royal Academy included his fourth large canal scene, *View on the Stour near Dedham*, and two Hampstead subjects. His fourth child, Isabel, was born on 23 August. Again actively engaged in making cloud studies at Hampstead. His connection with the French dealer John Arrowsmith began this year. He moved to 35 Charlotte Street and this remained his town house till his death.

1823   Constable's chief exhibit at the Royal Academy

was *Salisbury Cathedral from the Bishop's Grounds*. Visited Fisher in August and stayed with Sir George Beaumont at Coleorton from the last week of October until the end of November. On the latter visit he studied intensively his host's fine collection of Old Masters and made careful copies of two of his Claudes.

1824   His sole exhibit at the Royal Academy was his fifth large canal scene *The Lock*. *The Hay Wain*, the *View on the Stour near Dedham*, and a *View of Hampstead Heath* were exhibited at the Salon in Paris in this year. They were greatly acclaimed by the French artists, particularly Delacroix, and were awarded a gold medal by Charles X. Took his wife and family to Brighton for the first time in May, and himself spent some time in London and some with them in Brighton, returning at the end of August.

1825   Three paintings called 'Landscape' exhibited at the Royal Academy. One was the sixth large canal scene, *The Leaping Horse*, the other two being views of Hampstead Heath. His fifth child, Emily, was born on 29 March. *The White Horse* and another painting were exhibited at Lille; he was again awarded a gold medal.

1826   Exhibited at the Royal Academy *The Cornfield* and *A Mill at Gillingham in Dorsetshire*. His sixth child, Alfred Abram, was born on 14 November.

1827   *Chain Pier, Brighton*; *Mill Gillingham, Dorset*, and *Hampstead Heath* exhibited at the Royal Academy. *The Cornfield* exhibited at the Salon, whilst to the British Institution Constable sent a version of *The Glebe Farm*. He took John and Maria, his eldest children, for a holiday in Flatford with his

family in the autumn, and made a number of drawings. This year he took the house in Well Walk
which remained his Hampstead home till the end
of his life.

1828 Exhibited at the Royal Academy two paintings
called 'Landscape'. One was *Dedham Vale*, the
other was *Hampstead Heath*. His seventh child,
Lionel Bicknell, was born on 2 January. Constable
inherited a fortune from Maria's father, but his
wife's health was rapidly declining. He took her on
a last visit to Brighton in July, but she died in
Hampstead on 23 November, aged 41.

1829 Elected R.A. on 10 February. Exhibited *Hadleigh
Castle* and a landscape of a 'rich cottage' at the
Royal Academy. In this year he formulated his
plans for a series of mezzotints by David Lucas
after his paintings, later published as *English
Landscape Scenery*. Paid his last two visits to
Fisher at Salisbury in July and November.

1830 Constable was a member of the Hanging Committee of the Royal Academy, and in this year witnessed the rejection of his *Water-meadows near
Salisbury* as a 'nasty green thing'. His accepted
exhibits comprised views of Helmingham Park,
Hampstead Heath, and another landscape. The
first number of *English Landscape Scenery*, containing four plates, appeared in the summer.

1831 Exhibited *Salisbury Cathedral from the Meadows*
and *Yarmouth Pier* at the Royal Academy. Took
his daughter Maria to stay with his family in Suffolk in July, and later visited Mr Digby Neave at
Epsom.

1832 Showed the unusually large number of eight exhibits at the Royal Academy. The oils included

Waterloo Bridge from Whitehall Stairs, A Romantic House, Hampstead, and *Sir Richard Steele's Cottage, Hampstead.* The drawings included *Jaques and the Wounded Stag.* Constable's closest friend, Archdeacon John Fisher, died on 25 August. He was in East Bergholt in July and again for the funeral of his assistant John Dunthorne, son of his boyhood companion, in November.

1833   Among the four oil-paintings and three drawings exhibited at the Royal Academy were *Englefield House* and *The Cottage in a Cornfield.* Gave his first lecture on the history of landscape painting, at Hampstead. Made some drawings for an illustrated edition of Gray's *Elegy,* and spent a fortnight in October visiting his son John, who was at school in Folkestone.

1834   Constable had no oils at the Royal Academy this year, owing to illness. The three water-colours he showed included *Old Sarum.* Paid his first visit to George Constable at Arundel in July and stayed with Lord Egremont at Petworth in September; on both occasions he made many drawings and water-colours of the more rugged Sussex countryside.

1835   *The Valley Farm* (in the Tate Gallery) was his sole exhibit at the Royal Academy. Paid a second visit to George Constable in Arundel. In October went to Worcester, where he gave a lecture and made some drawings.

1836   This was the last occasion on which the Royal Academy's annual exhibition was held at Somerset House. Constable sent two works, *The Cenotaph* and the water-colour *Stonehenge.* Gave his lectures on the History of Landscape Painting in their definitive form at the Royal Institution in May and June.

1837   Died on 31 March. The day before his death he
       had been working on *Arundel Mill and Castle* in
       preparation for the Royal Academy, and it was
       shown posthumously at the first exhibition held at
       the National Gallery's building in Trafalgar
       Square.

1

EARLY YEARS IN THE CONSTABLE COUNTRY

THE Constable country is part of the valley through which the River Stour runs, and extends from Stratford St Mary in the county of Suffolk through Dedham to Manningtree on the Essex border. It is about two miles wide and six miles long, and the ridges which hem it in on either side rise to little more than 150 ft in height. These modest hills slope gently down to the river curving in the flat clay bottom. The contours of the hills are shallow convexities and concavities, and their plastic soil accounts for the assiduous meandering of the Stour. When, in later life, Constable wanted to give the engraver David Lucas an idea of the general character of the valley scenery he drew a diagram which is now in the Fitzwilliam Museum. Though it makes no profession of topographical accuracy, it shows clearly how with each bend of such a river a fresh viewpoint is reached. The artist's life-work lay in realizing the manifold variety latent in this small compass of land.

John Constable, who gives his name to this still beautiful tract of country, was born in the village of East Bergholt on 11 June 1776; his birthplace is on the crest of the northern ridge flanking the valley. For long before his birth the flat lands on the border of Essex and Suffolk, to which the Stour is at this point a boundary, had been intensively cultivated. At the end of the eighteenth century Essex was reputed to be one of the best-farmed counties in England, and Suffolk was not behindhand. Under the stimulus of the Continental wars an experimental attitude on the part of the landowners had led to a considerable gain in productivity, which was relevant indeed to Constable's career, even though this was mainly centred on London. The art of the landscape painter, which Constable adapted to the fertile terrain of his homeland, had been invented in the entirely different circumstances of the Burgundian Courts, and developed in the seventeenth century in the Roman Campagna. The basic facts of the land in which he was born, in which his father and brother worked, and which he loved with a single-minded affection all his life, are of vital importance for the understanding of Constable's art. Not only did these fields provide the financial pabulum which made him independent; they formed the most immediate subject of his thought and emotion. He never said a more revealing thing about himself than when he remarked of the Lake District 'the solitude of mountains oppressed his spirits'. He was only at home in a countryside in which the land was used for growing crops or feeding cattle, and in which men were engaged in these activities as their natural daily occupation. Though it may seem paradoxical it is hardly an exaggeration to call him an industrial landscape painter.

In the main the country in which Constable grew up was that sort of unpremeditated landscape garden formed by the agricultural labours of many generations. Husbandry is one of the few industries which can improve the raw materials of the Nature on which it depends. But one vital modern factor had been added to this valley in the seventeenth century. In 1628 Arnold Spencer obtained a patent authorizing him to make rivers navigable. When this came up for renewal in 1638 the instrument stated that, as well as improving the Great Ouse, Arnold Spencer had 'also provided for making navigable the river of Stour leading from Sudbury in the county of Suffolk to Manningtree in the county of Essex which is likely to prove no less commodious to the inhabitants of divers several towns in the said counties'; and it renews to him the authority 'to cut and make locks, sluices, bridges, cuts, dams and other inventions not repugnant to our laws'. This canalization of the River Stour provided the visible basis for Constable's art, and the list of Spencer's works is almost an inventory of his paintings. Although we may now think of canals as derelict watercourses, picturesque in decay, this and all the other canals of the early nineteenth century were thriving, busy concerns. Constable's father, who owned rights over the towpath, shipped his milled grain in barges from Dedham. When railway prospectors offered to buy the Stour canal at the outset of their expansion, in 1845, the owners were so confident of continuing prosperity that they held out for a far higher sum than was offered; and their profits did not seriously decline till the 1870s.

The lighters on the Stour were always hauled by horses in gangs of two barges, the front one of which alone contained a cabin. The towpath did not continuously follow one bank, and it was a custom individual to the Stour for the tow-horse to be ferried from one bank to the other on a barge – an incident illustrated by Constable in *The White Horse*. At other points the towpath was interrupted by barriers created to prevent cattle straying; the tow-horses were trained to leap over these obstacles, an action which is the theme of *The Leaping Horse*. The canal traffic was slow moving; it could in any case not have been borne on the roads, because they were in so frightful a state. So the tow-horses walked along the banks of the river and the lightermen on the barges steered their craft, which were moving at less than two miles an hour. On either side of the canal were the level, fertile water-meadows, and the upland fields used for pasture and for the ever-increasing crops of corn.

Essex ploughmen were famous for the perfection of their ploughing and the regularity of their furrows, and Constable constantly watched their skilful operations on the hillsides leading down to the river. Their plough was the common wheel plough, drawn by two horses, an instrument he has drawn with meticulous accuracy. When later he visited Worcester and Epsom he was still sufficiently interested in modern machinery to draw the regional variations in the type of plough. He would never tolerate imprecise observation of such implements.

Almost every natural object or group of objects seen by Constable near his home was the direct product of man's intervention with Nature. The trees cut back from the fields were shaped and placed by him, the division of the land, its hedges, fences, and lanes, even the course of the river, were under his control. The successive appearances of the fields, ranging rhythmically from the dark earth of winter through the young green of spring to the golden yellow of the harvest, were the product of man's mastery over natural powers. The mills, cottages, locks, and sluices which so delighted Constable were clearly man-made. Only the sky over all this land, the wide expanse of clouds characteristic of the flat coasts of East Anglia, was entirely capricious, and yet of vital importance to the culture of the country and to its appearance.

The qualities of the Essex–Suffolk border are as apparent in its negative as in its positive qualities. There are no wild gorges, high mountains, jagged rocks, emphatic contrasts; there is not even the glaring white of the exposed chalk seen elsewhere in Essex. But for Constable it was not anonymously pastoral; it was made personal to him by the sense of family ownership, and was mapped out by his father's possessions. Of the buildings which appear time and again in his pictures Flatford Mill, Dedham Mill, and Stratford Mill were his father's property; and Constable's paintings are suffused with this sense of proprietorship. He shared to the full that local sense of attachment to the soil of Suffolk which he exemplified to Lucas by a story recorded on the back of his valley diagram. This concerns a farm labourer in search of work who, after crossing the Stour to the Essex bank, looked back and said: 'Good-bye, old England, perhaps I may never see you more.'

Many budding artists discover their talent by seeing the paintings of other people; some are to be found with a chalk or pencil in their hands scribbling away before they have formulated any abstract ideas. The legend of Giotto and his O, the record of the boy Bewick in the mid-eighteenth century chalking on the gravestones and on the floor of the church porch, are examples of this precocious entrance into the artistic life. Constable, according to his own recollections, took another and more unusual path; he formulated his ideas by a power of visual imagination before he had any technical means for putting them on paper or canvas. He says of the scenes amid which he grew up: 'I had often thought of pictures of them before I had ever touched a pencil.' His obsession with the Stour Valley and the sights which 'made (him) a painter' remained with him all his life, and the progress of his painting consists in his rising ability to translate these earliest images of his boyhood imagination into the permanent forms of drawing or painting.

Constable was thus in a sense a *naïf* or intuitive painter, whose ideas preceded his ability to express them. Romanticism is sometimes reproached with making too much of the child, but childhood emotion recaptured and expressed with the means available to maturity is the basis of romantic art. In Constable, as with Bewick, the freshness and radiance, the untrammelled delight, which distinguish the innocent eye and the youthful imagination achieved their most effective expression when the child who had experienced them had reached the sophisticated calm of middle age.

However gifted a child may be, he must at some time meet a painter if he is going to express his exciting, hypnotic vision in permanent form. The artist who acts in this way as a technical guide and catalyst to the imagination of youthful genius need not himself be of the first rank. Coleridge was enraptured by the now forgotten sonnets of the Rev. William Lisle Bowles; Rembrandt was taught by Pieter Lastman. Chance provided for Constable in his small East Anglian birthplace a plumber and glazier, John Dunthorne, who was an enthusiastic amateur painter and became his close friend through this mutual interest. The tastes so awakened were judged and encouraged from the standpoint of cosmopolitan taste by Sir George Beaumont, who frequently visited his mother in her dower house in Dedham, and was eventually introduced to the young painter.

John Dunthorne was an independent, stubborn character and was not viewed with great favour by the villagers. Constable's mother criticized him for the way he had been chosen by his wife:

'to take in a man, from an advertisement, without a
change of raiment or a shilling in his pocket and marry
him ... surely he ought to be grateful at least'.

Constable's friendship with this social misfit caused him
some embarrassment at the crisis of his courtship of Maria
Bicknell, since Dunthorne was at loggerheads with the
rector of East Bergholt, Dr Rhudde, who was Maria's
grandfather. But it had been of the greatest importance to
Constable to share Dunthorne's interest in sketching, to hire
a studio with him and to be introduced by him to the
physical handling of paint when he was young and groping
for encouragement.

Sir George Beaumont was a really gifted amateur painter,
who was only not a professional because he was a wealthy
man. He had been taught by Alexander Cozens at Eton,
by J. B. Malchair at Oxford, and later on by Richard Wilson. A kindly, generous patron, he was the friend of Wordsworth and Coleridge, as well as their benefactor. His facility
and practical knowledge encouraged him in the appreciation of other painters' work, although even his magnanim-
ity was thwarted by the egocentricity of Haydon. His gift of
paintings by Claude and Rubens to the newly founded
National Gallery in 1824 was a decisive gesture in setting
the standard for its future. Two of the paintings included in
that gift had been of special importance to Constable. The
small upright Claude landscape 'Hagar and the Angel' was
in his possession when Constable first met him. Beaumont
so much admired this painting that he carried it in his
coach wherever he went. Constable's first sight of it, on one
of Beaumont's visits to Dedham, was an epoch in his life,
and its irrefutable effect upon his vision is shown by the
fact that his *Dedham Vale* of 1802 and the *Dedham Vale*
of 1828 repeat intrinsically the composition of that compact
and gem-like scene. Some years later, in 1803, Lady Beaumont gave her husband Rubens' 'Château de Steen'; and
the rich naturalism of that exuberant masterpiece was
echoed in the technique of Constable's maturity.

From Beaumont, Constable could hear a first-hand

account of two of the primordial masters of English landscape, Alexander Cozens and Richard Wilson. Through
him he may also have come to know of John Robert
Cozens, whom Beaumont helped, till his death in 1797, to
maintain in an asylum. Certainly he was shown the water-
colours of Thomas Girtin, and urged by Beaumont to imitate their breadth of handling. It was noticed as early as
1801 by Joseph Farington, the artistic know-all of his day,
that Constable's drawing of trees was indistinguishable
from Sir George Beaumont's. In fact, Beaumont acted on
Constable through his own painting, by the transmission of
the grand tradition, by the taste shown in his own collection, and as an exemplar of the polite world.

Before he came to Farington's notice, however, Constable had had instruction and guidance from yet other
sources. In 1796 he went to Edmonton to stay with relatives,
and there he fell in with John Thomas Smith, who was
engaged in the portrait painting which he described as 'I
profiled, three-quartered, full-faced and buttoned up the
retired embroidered weavers, their crummy wives, and
tight-laced daughters'.

J. T. Smith, who was born in a hackney carriage and died
in debt as Keeper of Prints and Drawings at the British
Museum, was in his own day of some account in the world
of art. He is no longer much remembered as a draughtsman
and etcher, but rather as a man of considerable character
and cockney appeal, and as a racy author. His father had
been assistant to Joseph Nollekens the sculptor, and after
practising himself some years as a sculptor had opened a
print shop; it was by this means that his son acquired his
considerable knowledge of the subject, and he was a constant attendant at auction sales. For Constable he embodied
the world of art at a lower but more practical level than
Beaumont, with a working knowledge of dealers, collectors,
and artists acquired through buying and selling. Furthermore he had an antiquarian obsession which impelled him
to seek and record the personal associations of the streets
and houses of London. His keen appreciation of eccentricity
is apparent in the anecdotes he records in A BOOK FOR A

RAINY DAY. For instance, he notes the habits of the man who had made a fortune in business, but who still got up at four o'clock in the morning to pick up the horseshoes which had been dropped during the night 'with no other notion than to see how many he could accumulate in a year'. This sense of the oddity of human behaviour, sharpened by the malice of the disappointed legacy hunter, gives his LIFE OF NOLLEKENS its timeless appeal. One of the earliest examples of candid biography, the book was reviled by Smith's contemporaries – even Haydon, who could be just as outspoken about people he detested, was outraged by it – but the detailed anatomy of its miserly and original subject gives the entertainment of barbed and original vision.

By the end of Smith's life – he died in 1833 – he and his pupil had drifted apart. Constable came to think poorly of his character, though with his innate kindness he lent him money he knew full well would never be returned, and raised a subscription for his indigent widow. This expressed his gratitude for the many valuable things he had learned from him when he was twenty. Smith encouraged his interest in prints, lending him etchings by Tempesta and Ruysdael to copy. He directed his reading towards the eighteenth-century theorists Algarotti and Gessner as well as the magisterial Leonardo da Vinci. He encouraged Constable to send him drawings of picturesque cottages for possible inclusion in the book REMARKS ON RURAL SCENERY which he was then preparing. In the event he did not make any etchings from Constable's rather scratchy drawings – they are among his earliest independent compositions – but the text with which he accompanies the plates is a summary of picturesque theory in which many of Constable's mature ideas and practices are to be seen in germ. In it Smith comments on the varieties and shades of green in Nature as a picturesque beauty resembling the scumble of moss and decay on a thatched roof, an idea which almost thirty years later Constable passed on to Delacroix, and of which his own paintings are a continual analysis. He followed, and repeated to Leslie, another precept of Smith's: 'Do not set about inventing figures for a landscape taken from Nature:

for you cannot remain an hour in any spot, however solitary, without the appearance of some living thing that will in all probability accord better with the scene and time of day than will any invention of your own.' *The Cottage in a Cornfield* provides just one instance of this, in the natural rightness of the magpie which has alighted on the path, the donkey tethered by the gate, and the white cat sitting on the garden fence.

Apart from the formal and technical instruction in art and art theory which he gave Constable, Smith had a wider influence on the course of his life. He encouraged him to consider becoming a professional artist at a time when his father opposed this step in favour of his entering the family mill. Furthermore, Smith's vivid sense of locality and its associations strengthened Constable's own love of the *genius loci*. His feeling that a place was rendered more interesting by its human links chimed in with Constable's own bent towards venerating the historical associations of his home country. This strengthened the concentration – almost the fanaticism – with which Constable devoured a particular place, the passion which is the central source of emotion in his painting.

Through Smith he met John Cranch, an artist of even more mediocre accomplishment, whose style Constable imitated in his first-known essays in oil-painting, deservedly forgotten. In this circle his veneration for Gainsborough was encouraged. No doubt with Constable this feeling originated in Gainsborough's own Suffolk birth and subject-matter, and his enthusiasm was also encouraged by Beaumont, Dr Monro, George Frost and other early friends. Constable wrote to Smith in 1799 from Ipswich: ''Tis a most delightful country for a landscape painter; I fancy I see Gainsborough in every hedge and hollow tree.'

Constable formed another friendship of far-reaching consequence during his country boyhood. The Rev. Brooke Hurlock, curate of the near-by parish of Langham, introduced him to Dr John Fisher, who had already embarked on the career of advancement at Court and in the Church which ended in his becoming Bishop of Salisbury. Fisher took a kindly interest in Constable throughout his life, though the recipient was sometimes irked by the element of patronage in this concern, and by his friend's old-fashioned taste in art.

So, when he finally left his father's business in 1799 to study art in London, Constable had learned the mechanics of painting from Dunthorne, the village amateur; he had admired Claude and Girtin in Sir George Beaumont's collection; and had received further instruction, including a knowledge of seventeenth-century Dutch landscape, from J. T. Smith. The theoretical education which he had so far acquired was conservative and conventional, biased towards the painting of historical, figure, and subject pictures and holding the view that art should generalize and not particularize. But Constable was a natural nonconformist, and did not long embrace any view inconsistent with his instincts; out of this conservative teaching he picked the signs which pointed to his future path – the detailed particularity of leaf-painting praised by Algarotti in Titian's 'St Peter Martyr', and Smith's indication of the countless tones which make up one patch of colour in Nature.

2

THE YEARS OF STUDY IN LONDON

THE artistic world of London was not in a dynamic state when Constable began to study in the Royal Academy in 1799. That institution, having been founded in 1768, was passing into the hands of the second generation of artists; but the moment was a dull one. History, or the subject painting of ancient themes, was still officially ranked as the highest class of art and was predominantly in the hands of the ageing President, Benjamin West, assisted by some perverse fireworks from Fuseli and more timid contributions from the new recruits, Howard and Thomson. Portrait painting, still the path to financial advance, was now led by the successors to Reynolds and Gainsborough; that is, Beechey, Hoppner, Opie, and Owen. Romney's powers were waning; Lawrence was emerging as the brilliant, if somewhat superficial, leader of the new generation. Yet the catalogue of the exhibition of the Academy in 1800 shows a surprising preponderance of landscape painting; surprising, that is, considering that it was rated below history and portrait painting. But in any case this work was old-fashioned in style, and the progressive modernity of the water-colourists (Girtin, Cotman, Varley) was not echoed in the oils of Sir Francis Bourgeois, 'Landscape Painter to the King', or those of T. Hofland – whom Constable later described as having 'sold a shadow of Gaspar Poussin for eighty guineas, and it is no more like Gaspar than the shadow of a man on a muddy road is like himself'. The more spirited and original work of S. W. Reynolds and R. R. Reinagle (both of whom became friends of Constable) awaits rediscovery today. The great exception was J. M. W. Turner, whose precocious talent had been recognized from the time he was first exhibited at the Academy when he was sixteen, in 1791.

Every generation contains the seeds of a revolt against

the previous one, and the first decade of the nineteenth century was to contain a movement which disposed of the lingering eighteenth-century tradition. From 1806 Wilkie, helped by Mulready and Jackson, and sporadically in association with Haydon, revivified subject painting with his return to Scottish peasant subject-matter, and the next thirty or forty years were dominated by him and his followers. But it was not Constable's destiny to be recognized as they were, in his early years. Apart from Turner, the contemporary leaders of landscape in popular esteem were Ward, Callcott, and Collins, and it took Constable more than twenty years to outstrip them.

In any case it needs a great deal of hindsight to see any signs of promise in the work Constable had done when he settled in London. A few wretched oils and scratchy drawings in inconsistent and derivative styles were all he had to show. His powers at their fullest stretch can be judged from the four drawings he made as a wedding present for his boyhood friend Lucy Hurlock on her marriage in 1800. The sketching-point he chose, near Stratford Bridge, was one to which he returned again and again. His absorbed concentration on every visible detail in these scenes anticipates the passion for descriptive accuracy in his maturest work, reflecting the phrase in a letter he wrote to Dunthorne in the same year: 'I even love every stile and stump, and every lane in the village, so deep rooted are early impressions.' But the style in which these immensely painstaking labours of love are drawn and tinted is a weak and exhausted version of the eighteenth-century topographical manner. It comes as no surprise to find that one of them, when acquired by the Whitworth Art Gallery, Manchester, was attributed to the Swiss water-colourist Michael Vincent Brandoin.

The attractiveness of his character and his evident determination to succeed must have weighed more with his examiners than the actual work he could present when he was accepted as a student. And he owed something to his fortune in being introduced to Joseph Farington at the time of his application. Farington as a painter was a secondary pupil of Richard Wilson's, but there was little in his tired and formal schemata to fire the imagination of a lively student. As a personality he was far more considerable, a consummate example of those figures who exist in most developed artistic societies, the art politicians: in this case the 'Dictator' of the Royal Academy. The centre of gossip and intrigue, he knew most of what was going on, and ambitious young men came to him to know their chances of election as A.R.A. or R.A. and for prudent, worldly or technical advice. Although their characters, no less than their artistic aims, were so different, Constable and Farington got on well. Farington gave genuine help to Constable, who repaid it with a permanent feeling of respect for the cold handsome man, of commanding presence, who so much valued his position as *éminence grise*.

Benjamin West, the President of the Royal Academy, was also a somewhat unexpected source of encouragement and technical advice. In later years Constable did not trouble to conceal his contempt for West's paintings. 'West is only hanging on by the tail of the Shirt of Carlo Maratti and the fag-end of the Roman and Bolognese schools – the last of the Altorum Romanorum, and only the shadow of them', and he dismissed the whole tradition of English history painting in which he worked as 'preferring the shaggy posteriors of a Satyr to the moral feeling of landscape'. None the less, West had seen the genuine feeling for nature in Constable's early ineffectual painting, and gave him a practical lesson in drawing which he always remembered. Looking at a rejected painting, he touched in some lights between the stems and branches of the trees with chalk, saying: 'Always remember, sir, that light and shadow never stand still.' He also taught Constable that in his lowering skies his darks should look like the darks of silver, not of lead or slate. Again, when he was offered an appointment as drawing master, West dissuaded him from taking it, and explained the reasons to its protagonist, Dr Fisher, whom Constable was afraid of offending by a refusal.

His curriculum as a student included the familiar one of drawing from the life and from casts, in which he achieved no remarkable results. He was fascinated by the anatomy lessons, as he was by astronomy, and this insight into structure is part of the underlying culture of his mind. Leslie praises the coloured drawings of dissections he did at this time, but these are not apparently now known. More relevant to his future career was the course of copying he set himself; at this time he copied Claude, Rubens, Poussin, and throughout his life he maintained the practice.

The eight years which followed Constable's admission as a student were a time of experiments and false starts. While he was working extremely hard to make up for the arrears in his technical training he made a number of excursions in the traditional moulds of the artist's life. In doing so he made mistakes, but he rarely made the same type of mistake again. His obstinacy and self-knowledge enabled him to return to the line of development which was for him a personal necessity; the underlying themes of this strangely tentative early career are his determination to be original, and his instinct for rejecting all but a narrow line of advance. The native school of landscape painting had grown up from the demands of English landowners for portraits of their houses and grounds. At the beginning of the nineteenth century accordingly, it was still resistant to a sense of the *genius loci*. Just as the portrait painter accepted almost any sitter in his studio, the landscape painter must be ready to travel anywhere to take a prospect or render a view. Constable's work was to prove one of the steps which liberated landscape towards the expression of a mood, an aim crystallized in Impressionism. But side by side with universality in subject-matter had gone the recognition of certain special areas which were 'beauty spots'. Wales, the Peak District of Derbyshire, the Lake District, were British examples to set beside the Alps, the Roman Campagna and some medieval German and Austrian towns. When Constable set out on a picturesque sketching tour of the Peak District in 1801 he was following a well-established Romantic route. In the three weeks or so that he spent there he sketched the main views – Matlock High Tor, Mam Tor, Chatsworth, Haddon Hall. The style aims at being bold

and descriptive, and form is given to the flaccid pencil outlines by grey washes of varied depths of tone; but the level
of competence hardly rises above that of Paul Sandby
Munn, Thomas Sutherland or other forgotten artists of the
time. In fact, the resemblance between Constable's style and
Sir George Beaumont's, noted by Farington in the oil-
painting *Old Hall, East Bergholt* of this year, is even more
apparent in these drawings of the Peak District. In the next
year, 1802, Constable went to East Bergholt in a spirit of
self-examination with results far more important than his
alien sketching tours, and these must be described in more
detail below.

His next considerable journey away from East Anglia
was partly sea-borne. In April 1803 he boarded the East
Indiaman *Coutts*, whose captain was a friend of his father.
Suiting his style to the nautical turn of his subjects, his
drawings this time were made in close imitation of Van de
Velde. In this manner he made over 100 studies of the shipping in the Thames and the Medway. He also walked over-
land from Gravesend to Rochester and Chatham, making
further drawings on his way. From these sketches he subsequently formulated one ambitious work – the large water-
colour of 'H.M.S. *Victory* ... in the memorable battle of
Trafalgar' which he exhibited at the Royal Academy in
1806. The subject was one which had a good deal of
personal significance for him, since the battle had been
described to him by a Suffolk man; but none of this involve-
ment is apparent in the gloomy, faded imitation of Girtin
which is now in the Victoria and Albert Museum. It was
clearly not Constable's destiny to be a marine painter in the
tradition of Van de Velde, Monamy, Scott, and Brooking;
when, eighteen years later, the British Institution offered
prizes for the best pictures of Trafalgar and the Nile he
wrote: 'It does not concern me much.' Yet he was always
fascinated with boats as practical working pieces of
machinery; his study of the Stour barges was unending, and
he was careful to note the different forms of the fishing-
boats at Hastings and Brighton. His more successful contact with the sea in fact began when he went to Brighton in

1824 and made his series of dazzling oil sketches. Even so he was reluctant to elaborate them into larger compositions; 'these subjects are so hackneyed in the Exhibition'. In between these successive waves of influence – J. T. Smith, Van de Velde, Girtin, Beaumont – came a short period when his drawings show that he had Gainsborough strongly in mind.

The most sustained attempt he made at forcibly broadening his subject-matter was also in 1806, when he spent nearly two months in the Lake District at the expense of his uncle, David Pike Watts. He stayed for some days at Brathay Hall, the home on Windermere of Mrs Harden. From the diary she was luckily keeping we can get a good impression of the impact Constable made at this time; his energy in constantly sketching, his musical interests, his artistic exhibitionism. It was with this visit to the Lakes in mind that Constable said later that the 'solitude of mountains oppressed his spirits'; yet while he was engaged upon it it was more nearly a success than any other of the sketching tours he made for conventional reasons. The forty or so water-colours which survive from the journey have a quality of gloomy power well suited to the romantic, vertiginous horrors of the hills. They are fine, expressive interpretations of their subject, yet in a sense they are not the work of the artist we know as 'Constable'; they are survivals from the posterity of Cozens and Girtin. In them is seen the final appearance of Beaumont's direct effect on Constable's style (Beaumont himself made one of his extensive tours of the Lakes in 1806). When the artist wrote on a view of Borrowdale 'tone very mellow like the mildest of Gaspar Poussin and Sir George Beaumont' he showed that he was mindful of this influence. In consequence the water-colours are conceived in a warm monochrome, and make no attempt at the truth of natural colour which he had already sought in oil-painting. But, untypical though they are, there are signs in his Lake District sketches of his maturer methods. It was on them that he first began to write systematic notes of the prevailing weather. This recognition of the importance of atmosphere and climate to his own art was a decisive advance. Although not so technically meteorological as his notes on the Hampstead sky studies of 1821 and 1822, they embody detailed observation. In early October he writes: 'Dark Autumnal day at noon – tone more blooming than this – the effect exceeding terrific and much like the beautiful Gaspar I saw in Margaret Street' (Margaret Street was then a haunt of dealers' shops). Other effects he notices are 'morning previous to a fine day' (a clever rendering of shafts of sunlight casting shadows on the valley mist); 'twilight after a very fine day'; 'noon clouds breaking away after rain'; 'the finest scenery that ever was'. The tone of these comments contrasts oddly with his later disparagement; in fact, the enthusiasm they reflect lasted for three years, and he was still sending paintings of Lake District subjects to the Royal Academy in 1809. The drawings represent his most Wordsworthian moment, and he did, in fact, meet Wordsworth at this time, though the meeting was not a great success; Constable thought the poet held too high an opinion of himself. The water-colours emphasize the claustrophobic, frightening aspects of mountains, the quality felt in Wordsworth's paranoiac lines about Ullswater

'the huge Cliff
Rose up between me and the stars, and still,
With measured motion, like a living thing,
Strode after me.'

In sharp contrast with the drawings, the few oil sketches which are known to come from his Lake District journey are not a dead end in his development, but show the birth of characteristics which matured in his Suffolk scenes from 1809 onwards. *Keswick Lake*, in the Paul Mellon Collection, is a good example. For the first time a freedom of brushwork and brilliance of colour foreshadowing the *View of Dedham Vale* and *A cart on a road near East Bergholt* can be seen. These qualities somewhat alarmed his friends, no doubt giving the impetus to Mrs Harden's feeling that he was painting too much for effect.

These years of groping showed also that it was not in

Constable to become a painter of religious subjects. He owed his commissions for altar-pieces to local interest in his career; and even so they were only three in number. For Brantham Church he undertook in 1805 a composition of eight figures, *Christ blessing the Children*. This was his most elaborate attempt in the uncongenial field of history painting; it was conceived in close dependence on the style of Benjamin West, and though Constable's great fondness for children can be felt in it, no one has ever considered it a success. In 1810 he painted a simpler composition, *Christ blessing the Bread and Wine*, for Nayland Church: this was confined to the single figure of Christ. His only other attempt was made in 1822, when a distant cousin presented an altar-piece, *The Ascension*, to the church at Manning-tree – in order to assist the licensing of his public houses.

Another uncongenial domain upon which Constable tried to enter was portrait painting. In this he persevered more consistently; nearly 100 portraits by him are known. At the outset he was under great pressure to develop this side of his career. Like so many English families in their position, Constable's parents were acutely aware of the value of respectability. Their son, John, had failed in two methods of achieving that respectability: first, he had not gone into the Church; secondly, he had not followed his father's career. But the danger he ran by becoming an artist could be redressed if he became a fashionable portrait painter. Wilson was not respectable; he was fond of the bottle and died poor. On the other hand, Lawrence, who was constantly in financial straits, was undoubtedly respectable, and his parents wished John Constable to follow this model. So he dutifully fagged away, at first painting the local farmers and their wives; but to him portraiture was always 'a job' and he never entered into its spirit. Occasionally he was successful; as in his landscape painting, this happened when he felt a special sympathy with his subject. His portraits of his sisters, of Maria Bicknell, who became his wife, of Greswold Lewis, are of this calibre; the others are generally undistinguished. But the time he spent on these thankless tasks was not all wasted; from it he derived an insight into technique and a facility of execution without which, as he himself recognized, he could not have developed as a land-scape painter.

Up till 1808 – that is, until he was 32 – Constable had been serving a long self-imposed apprenticeship. The valu-able product of those years, seen in the perspective of his main development, comprises a small number of brilliant, fresh and novel landscape sketches of Dedham Vale, with a few water-colours of East Bergholt Church. Against these have to be put a mass of studies of the academic nude, derivative sketches of the Peak District, a number of in-different portraits, a bad altar-piece, a number of intense water-colours of the Lake District which are nevertheless not the work he wished to accomplish, and a minute number of brilliant oil sketches of the same scenery. If there is any question to be asked about an artist more futile than 'What would he have accomplished had he not died?' it is 'What would our opinion of him have been had he died young?' But there is an answer to the latter question, and in Con-stable's case we can state it fairly precisely. Bonington died, with a considerable English and European reputation, in his late twenties. By contrast, had Constable died in his early thirties he would have been unknown outside the small circle of his friends. He might have been rediscovered as a person of individual character in the mid-twentieth century; but whether any inkling of his real genius could have been divined would depend entirely on the survival of a few exceptional paintings, the product of his withdrawal to East Bergholt in 1802.

These works in which he announced the future were created in hours of deliberate and obstinate recollection in his home county. The impetus which led to their creation came from his sudden realization that his friends in London – and specifically Reinagle – were not sufficiently honest in purpose. It had been natural, even essential, for Constable to copy Claude, Poussin, Rubens, Van de Velde, Reynolds; without this exercise he could not have mastered the techni-que of painting in oils. But Reinagle not only produced pastiches of these artists as his own work; he painted deliberate forgeries of them. The realization that these practices were current came as a shock to Constable's absolute integrity. It led to the letter he wrote to Dunthorne in 1802 about his artistic intentions, the letter in which he made the famous and prophetic self-revelation: 'For these two past years I have been running after pictures and seeking the truth at secondhand. I have ... endeavoured to make my performance look as if really *executed* by other men ... I shall shortly return to Bergholt where I shall make some laborious studies from nature ... there is room enough for a natural painter.' On this he went down to East Bergholt and put his resolution into effect. Some of the oil sketches he made in 1802 with these clear-sighted intentions are known; four of them, including the upright *Dedham Vale*, are in the Victoria and Albert Museum and two are in the Paul Mellon Collection. They are remarkable productions both in the context of their time and in relation to Constable's other work at this date. The inwardness of feeling which pervades his Stour scenes begins to appear. They are natural, and naturalistic, studies of the scenes in front of his eyes, without any undue striving to adapt them to the formulae of eighteenth-century compositions. To an extent, it is true, they are new wine in old bottles; the range of colour-matching is not so bold or extensive as it became ten years later, and the skies are straightforward, almost like that 'white sheet thrown behind the objects' scorned by Constable in later years. But he was already reaching out for some of his classic formulations of the structure of the Stour Valley and its appearance under the light of a summer evening or an autumn morning. The upright view of Dedham Vale shows, from a viewpoint on Gun Hill, the long winding course of the River Stour on its way to the estuary at Manningtree and Harwich. This composition, which is in a way a rediscovery in Nature of the design of Sir George Beaumont's favourite Claude, 'Hagar and the Angel', recurs with variations throughout his life and reaches its most elaborated form in the *Dedham Vale* of 1828 in the National Gallery of Scotland.

Even after this advance in oil-painting, in the drawings he

made in Suffolk and Essex he still wavered between more than one style, being sometimes influenced by Gainsborough and at other times by Girtin. Not till he embarked on a series of luminous water-colours of East Bergholt Church from 1806 did he begin to introduce the light reds and stone greys which were to banish the heavy monochrome of the style he had used – in the same year – for Lake District scenes.

So the years from 1799 till 1808 saw a dispersed, and to some extent ineffectual, but highly energetic entrance by Constable upon the career of a professional artist. He had learned the technique of his art thoroughly, and the excellent condition of his paintings today shows how sound that preparation was. He had also come to a clear understanding of his own genius. With him, to limit his scope was to increase his capacity beyond all proportion. Though never entirely free of commissions which harassed him he more and more concentrated on painting the pictures he had dreamed of as a child playing on the banks of the Stour. On his future travels he painted only where he was a welcome guest, where he could gradually grow into the feeling of the landscape as an intimate, not as a casual tourist. In this deliberate way he absorbed Salisbury, Osmington, Hampstead, Arundel, into his repertory of paintable places.

3

FIRST SIGNS OF MASTERY: 1809–16

FROM 1809 onwards there were virtually no more false starts and abandoned experiments in Constable's work. He was still confronted by the indifference of the public, and his private life was far from composed till his marriage to Maria Bicknell in 1816, but after his visit to the Lakes his work went serenely and confidently forward. The portraits he still painted from time to time no longer disturbed the even progress of his style in landscape painting. He had realized that he must limit his range to intensify his effect, and never retreated from this position. From now on virtually every painting he made is recognizably 'a Constable'; there are few irrelevant digressions, and his drawings and oil sketches are means towards an end which he had fully understood and clearly defined to himself.

A number of related factors which helped towards this sudden emancipation might be found. In 1809 Farington had criticized his largest Lake District painting as 'wanting colour and effect', and this, chiming with his own realization of its lack of inwardness, may have acted as a corrective. The copies of portraits by Reynolds he had made for Lord Dysart had certainly given him a new facility in the technique of oil painting. This was the 'fagging at execution' of which he had written to Dunthorne, and which bore such good fruit in the excellence of his handling: while Turner's paintings are a constant problem to the restorer, Constable's have remained in excellent condition. It is one of the fascinations of a closer study of his work to see in detail his progression in facility and impressiveness from the liquid suavity and calm colour of the *Dedham Vale* of 1811 to the broken accents and harsher rhythms of *The Leaping Horse*, painted some fourteen years later.

Constable had already shown, in the naturalistic pieces he had painted in 1802 – described at the end of the previous chapter – that he was more relaxed in the scenery of his homeland, and therefore more capable of experiment with this material. So it comes as no surprise to find that his new expansion of knowledge, his new confidence and energy, first manifest themselves in small oil sketches of the fields within walking distance of his home at East Bergholt. From 1809 he painted an increasing number of these open-air oil sketches of small size – they show how he was able to embody more rapidly and more fully the visual images of this landscape which had been imprinted on his mind since childhood. These sketches are marked by the confidence and fluidity of their treatment and by the fact that they are virtually more naturalistic than any sketches made before. Their only competitors in freshness of vision are, as Sir Kenneth Clark has pointed out, those made by Turner at almost the same date.

The precise features of the greater naturalism of Constable's new style require some definition. He had already painted, in the *Dedham Vale* and its companions of 1802, pictures as advanced in this direction as any hitherto seen; they are natural and unaffected in composition and convey the sense of a scene bathed in a unifying light. None the less, the colour range is not wide; in the *Dedham Vale* of 1802 the scale varies from the light blue of the sky through the green of the trees' foliage to the grey-brown of the trunks and the light red of the distant roofs of Dedham, with an occasional sharper accent, such as the white of the clouds and of the sails in the distant estuary. Perhaps this study was left unfinished, but the foreground is the conventional brown ground, not painted on further, of the primed canvas; the trees cast little shadow, and there is no correlation between sky and shadow, as some of the blue and white of the sky appears amidst the foliation of the right-hand tree, which is somewhat flimsy in structure. The painting, delightful and satisfying as it is, looks backwards towards Wilson and Gainsborough rather than forwards towards the later nineteenth century; in spite of West's advice, light and shade do appear in it to stand still.

The sketch *A cart on a road near East Bergholt*, dated

1811, reveals an entirely different method of handling and approach. Painted over a slightly redder ground, the blue of the sky is brighter, the green of the foliage varies, according to the shade on the trees and grass, from dark grey-green to light yellowish-green; the walls of the mill buildings are a warm red-brown. An almost harsh note is struck by the rich red at the front of the cart. The colour grows in intensity by being isolated in thick emphatic strokes, and altogether the effect is of a more violent apprehension of the scene than in the study painted nine years before. In his approach to form in all the sketches of this period Constable conceives the Stour Valley like a concave sculptural object of which he fully understands the plastic construction, by intimate knowledge of every detail in it.

He did not now seek to represent this country under the one unified, serene form of lighting which he had caught so well in the painting of 1802; his new work is consistent with the intense heat of a spring day which casts the leaves into a dark shadow. In the sketch of *Barges on the Stour* which was probably painted at about the same time he shows his sensitiveness to a stormy autumn light. The prepared ground on which the sketch is painted is browner, the sky is dark grey-blue, lit with a sickly yellow cloud, and the meadows are a corresponding yellow-green. The grey of the lock's posts and the light blue of the smoke from the barge going through the lock help to complete an unusual pattern of colours which show how far Constable has come in some eight or ten years in developing his perception of the effect of changing atmospheric conditions on the tones of the scenery. A corresponding subtlety of perception and rendering can be seen in all his sketches of this time – the *View of Dedham Vale*, the *Country Lane near Flatford*.

Although there is a sense of completeness and fulfilment about the sketches of this period, they do not reflect a corresponding order in his life. In 1809, when he was 33, he had met Maria Bicknell for the first time since her childhood; he courted her against her family's opposition for the next seven years. Maria was the granddaughter of Dr Rhudde, the rector of East Bergholt, from whom she had expectations; her father, Charles Bicknell, was Solicitor to the Admiralty. This correlation of money and official position seems to have imbued the rector and his son-in-law with a more than normal concern for respectability and position, with the result that they strenuously discouraged a match between Maria and the son of a mill-owner who was an impecunious artist. Local village politics also contributed to their opposition; John's father, Golding Constable, had fallen foul of Dr Rhudde; John himself was said to have made a caricature of him; John Dunthorne, Constable's close friend, was the village atheist. In spite of this powerful opposition, Constable pursued his courtship with the tenacity that he applied to his painting and with the same eventual, though belated, success. The courtship followed unemphatic lines, like the plot of a Jane Austen novel, but a deep and lasting passion burns in the stereotyped and conventional phrases of the letters the two lovers wrote to one another.

In these years of continual study Constable followed a fairly regular routine. He could spend the late autumn, winter and early spring in London, working up his sketches from Nature and preparing his paintings for the Royal Academy exhibition, which began each May. Then he would go down to East Bergholt for an eagerly awaited release from town life in the summer and early autumn. Occasionally he broke the routine by making visits to his friends. A particularly important epoch in his life was marked by the journey he made to Salisbury in 1811 at the invitation of his old friend and adviser Dr Fisher, now Bishop of this see. It was Constable's first trip there, during which, in all probability, he met the Bishop's nephew John Fisher, who became his closest friend and whose support was of the greatest help to him during the troubles of his engagement. Constable did not exaggerate when he once wrote: 'Believe me, my dear Fisher, I should almost faint by the way when I am standing before my large canvases, were I not cheered and encouraged by your friendship and approbation.' Of the long correspondence with Fisher in which Constable poured out his innermost thoughts as though in the confessional it will be time to speak later. The visit to Salisbury had another importance, since it provided Constable, for the first time, with scenes which he could paint with the same feelings of intimate affection as those he felt primordially for the borders of Essex and Suffolk. After an unusually short period of gestation he was able to proceed from his first Salisbury drawings, made in 1811, to the painting of a *View of Salisbury*, now in the Louvre, which was much praised when he exhibited it at the Royal Academy in 1812. This year his paintings were unusually well hung. When Constable asked Benjamin West if he thought his method of study was the right preparation for future excellence the President replied: 'Sir, I consider that you have attained it.' The Salisbury scene fructified in his mind and was to form one of his major themes, as important as Hampstead, more so than Brighton and Arundel.

In 1815 and 1816 his visits to East Bergholt became more frequent and prolonged, because the health of his parents, to whom he was deeply attached, was failing. His mother died early in 1815, in her sixty-seventh year; his father survived her for just over a year, and was seventy-seven when he died. With a genuine grief this double event brought emancipation to their son. His share of the family wealth enabled him to marry Maria Bicknell, and the happiness the marriage brought him was the prelude to his most mature, concentrated, and productive period of painting.

Something must be said here about the other members of Constable's family to explain the basis of his new security. He had three brothers and three sisters. The eldest boy, Golding Constable, was somewhat mentally retarded; being unfit for the family business he found his main occupation in shooting, and eventually became gamekeeper to Lady Dysart. Only one of his sisters married; this was Martha, the second born, who married Nathaniel Whalley. The eldest girl, Ann, was a somewhat Amazonian character; Mary, much younger, was a gentler and weaker person who ultimately became absorbed in genealogical research into the family pedigree. Once John Constable had defected to his art there only remained to carry on the family business the last-born brother Abram, and to him Golding Constable left the entire concern in trust for the others.

Vincent van Gogh's brother, Theo, rightly occupies a high place in the annals of men who have unselfishly devoted themselves to fostering artistic genius in others. Abram Constable deserves to be no less highly regarded for the service he performed for his brother John. Although of a worrying and hypochondriacal disposition, he undertook the entire management of the mills and ungrudgingly supplied John with his share of the profits which accrued to his care and prudence. He took a great pride in his brother's rising fame, and relatively glittering London life, but himself discreetly avoided the perils of marriage. Nor was his management of the business a mere formality. He took control at the very time when the end of the Napoleonic wars had started the worst phase of agricultural distress. Only by good sense, skill, and his excellent judgement of quality in grain was he able to thrive as he did. His diligence provided the hard cash which enabled his brother to continue painting in London without many commissions, and so to work out his destiny.

Reviewing in more detail the production of these seminal years, 1809 to 1816, we see that his work comprises a great many sketches in oil and pencil made in the presence of the motif, and all conceived as preparations for more elaborately finished oil-paintings: these fully-worked-out oil-paintings were, however, relatively few in number and small in size. It was always the artist's desire to send his ambitious paintings to the annual exhibition at the Royal Academy. The exhibited works accordingly chart the progress of his intentions. In the eight years from 1809 to 1816 he exhibited twenty-five works, twenty-two of which were in oil. We can no longer say for certain in every case which paintings these were, but we can identify a representative selection, and these help to trace the curve of his interests and the rising confidence of his style. For instance, we can point to *East Bergholt Church* in the Tate Gallery, exhibited in 1810; *Dedham Vale: Morning* in the collection of Sir Richard Proby, exhibited in 1811; *Flatford Mill*, recently

shown in an American collection, and exhibited in 1812
with the *View of Salisbury*; a *Lock on the Stour*, the composition of which is known from a mezzotint, exhibited in
1813; *A Summerland* in the Paul Mellon Collection and
The Mill Stream at Ipswich, which were exhibited in 1814;
Boatbuilding near Flatford Mill, exhibited in 1815, the year
in which he finished a view of Dedham Vale, *Stour Valley
and Dedham Village*, now in Boston, painted as a wedding
present for Miss Philadelphia Godfrey.

With all the impression of steady progress there are
cross-currents of style within these years. Sir Richard
Proby's *Dedham Vale* is the first completely successful
embodiment in paint of his feeling for his countryside. It
has all the freshness of confident enthusiasm, and embodies
the serenity of a summer morning with the naturalness of
effect which he had set himself to master. He said this work
had cost him more trouble than any other, and certainly he
put into the task all he had learned from his casual and
inspired open-air sketches. It is a studied construction (the
left-hand tree is an obvious compositional device) which
has not lost verisimilitude, and a work of many months
which has not become laboured. The acuity of distant vision
is one of the most apparent features of Constable's rendering of the valley; and it may be noticed that this is not only
a new feature which he introduced into landscape painting
in contrast to the generalized particulars of the eighteenth-
century school; it is also consistent with the light of a
summer morning which forms the sub-title of the picture.
For in that warm air near the sea the visibility would be
unimpaired. This is an early instance of the correlation between sky and landscape which Constable studied ever
more deeply as he progressed in experience. In contrast to
the seemingly effortless naturalism of this piece some of his
sketches of 1812 are painted in a richly coloured, flowing,
linear style which shows that he has recently looked again
at Rubens.

It will be seen that, with the exception of the *View of
Salisbury* shown in 1812, the scenes of these paintings are
all within a child's walking range of the Constables' home,

and that in many of them the mill property owned by
Golding Constable features as viewpoint or as subject-
matter. The obsession which transformed John Constable
from an eclectic amateur to a great painter is in full play;
and the obsession can be seen still more clearly in the
range of his sketches and drawings from these eight years.

For Constable 1813 was an *annus mirabilis*. It was long
recalled as the year of the most bountiful harvest in living
memory. Day after day the sun shone and the Stour Valley
was bright, fertile, and busy with work. By a remarkable
conjunction of circumstances Constable came to his homeland, in this year of marvellous weather, in a peculiarly
receptive state of mind. He was deeply in love with Maria
Bicknell, but separated from her, and the obstacles to their
marriage then seemed insurmountable. His only remedy
for this agony of mind was his work, and he plunged into it
with an absolute abandon. This work mainly took the form
of walking in the countryside, reflecting upon it, recreating
his perception of it and recording it in a small pocket
sketch-book. Most fortunately his sketch-book has remained
intact, and is in the Victoria and Albert Museum. It is, more
than any one other single object, a unique record of Constable's creative power at work. Its dated pages cover more
than three months, from 10 July till 22 October, and show
him at work almost daily and at all times of the day; his
sketches show the corn standing thick in the fields on 13
July.

The state of mind in which he composed these gem-like
drawings was defined by a remark he made to Maria: 'I
believe we can do nothing worse than indulge in a useless
sensibility – but I can hardly tell you what I feel at the sight
from the windows where I am now writing of the fields in
which we have so often walked.' The intensity with which
he sketched in this long glaring summer was comparable
with that of two years before, of which he said: 'I almost
put my eyes out by that practice.'

In this small book, the leaves of which measure only
$3\frac{1}{2} \times 4\frac{3}{4}$in., seventy-two pages are drawn upon; but, since
many of these contain more than one miniature, precisely

detailed sketch, the number of individual acts of concentrated vision it records, for the fifteen weeks in which he
used it, is 132. Every one of these – and some of them are
quite literally 'thumbnail sketches' – is a crystallization of
the scene before him, and in sum they reveal more clearly
than any other evidence the intensity of purpose which was
linked with his narrowness of range. Almost all the local
themes which he used in his paintings are here seen from
different viewpoints and at different times of day; East
Bergholt Church, Stoke-by-Nayland Church, Flatford Mill,
Bridge Cottage and Flatford Bridge, Dedham Vale. Of
some of these subjects he had already formulated very
similar treatments; of the view of Dedham from Langham,
for instance, which became the basis of one of the most
typical mezzotints in ENGLISH LANDSCAPE SCENERY, he had
already made an oil sketch in 1812. He used the book when
he was planning a number of other later works, for instance
Flatford Mill and *The Valley Farm.*

The importance which the actual working life of the
countryside had for Constable has been emphasized and is
corroborated by the variety of occupations which have
caught his eye in this ruminative passage through the fields.
Thus we find pages showing a boy poling a barge, used as
a note for the *View on the Stour near Dedham* at San
Marino; studies of a man ploughing, used in *A Summerland*; as well as representations of reaping, of threshing, of
countrymen walking in the fields and of a tow-horse drawing a barge. Constable used the book, much in the way
Watteau had used his volumes of figure drawings, as an
index for ideas when he was composing on a grander scale.
In all the sketches, however minute, his thorough knowledge
of the entire plastic construction of the Stour Valley is
evident; he encompasses all the detail he sees and knows, all
these well-known shapes and objects, in a concave spider's
web of soft pencil line, a cat's cradle of acutely realized
form. From now on Constable's drawing merits equal attention with his paintings. In his tree drawings alone – for instance, *Fir Trees* – he combines in a unique way his acuity
of vision and accuracy of observation with a passion for the

natural object before his eyes. They are embodiments of that feeling which Leslie records: 'I have seen him admire a fine tree with an ecstasy of delight like that with which he would catch up a beautiful child in his arms.'

In 1814 he kept up another sketch-book which is as intimate and revealing as the great one of 1813, but is markedly different in manner. The page size is slightly smaller – 3⅛ × 4½in. – and only fifty-eight leaves are drawn upon, giving about eighty-one different sketches in all. The summer and autumn it records were more unsettled in weather than the previous year; whether for this reason, or through a deliberate plan, the drawings are bolder and far more concerned with broad effects of light and shade than were those of 1813. It is remarkable what force and vivacity, especially in his skies, Constable succeeds in achieving in this discouraging compass. Many of the drawings are directly connected as compositional or figure studies with the *Stour Valley and Dedham Village* at Boston; the composition and figure studies for *Boatbuilding near Flatford Mill* are here; and the book also contains the germ of the *View on the Stour near Dedham* and drawings used in *The White Horse*, and his compositions based on Stoke-by-Nayland Church. The two books together contain a remarkable repertory of his favourite subjects, and show the precipitating effect the combination of emotion, tension, and absorbed reflection had on him.

As the result of this intensive research into the small area of his choice Constable was by 1815 fully equipped with a minutely detailed knowledge of the land. He had all the materials on which to base his more ambitious paintings of the Stour Valley. Novelty in future would come from the development of his style, from the increasing ambition of his efforts and from the enlargement of his subject-matter to include Hampstead, Brighton, Osmington, Salisbury, and Arundel.

This phase of development, of early experiment, and of his first mastery was terminated in 1816 by his marriage to Maria Bicknell, which happily ended the acute emotional strain under which he had been living. His late autumn honeymoon in Dorset introduced him to a new scene and heralded a short but productive interlude in his career. John Fisher, who was himself newly wed, married them on 2 October and invited them to spend their honeymoon at his vicarage at Osmington in Dorset. Travelling easily, the Constables set out by way of Southampton and visited Netley Abbey on their way. They took perhaps a fortnight to reach their destination, which is on the downs overlooking Weymouth Bay. Here Constable made a number of drawings of the wild and attractive coastline dominated by Portland Island and the Chesil Bank. Even here the scene already had some personal associations, because his cousin had been shipwrecked and drowned on the Chesil Bank in the ship *Falconer.* He also made on this visit a number of small oil sketches which he left with John Fisher, and a sketch of Weymouth Bay under a tempestuous November sky which became the basis of two larger and later compositions, one of which is in the Louvre and the other in the National Gallery. This was the most westerly point he reached on the South Coast, and its productions are unusual in Constable's work both for the places they represent and in their being transcriptions of November weather by the sea.

4

THE LARGE CANAL SCENES

THE intensive work of preparation which Constable had undertaken was now sufficient to yield results. He had no intention of resting his reputation on small landscape sketches, however truthful, which stayed unseen in his studio, or on small finished paintings which, when shown at the Royal Academy, failed to attract attention through their absence of exaggerated effect. When writing about the crisis of Constable's long engagement Leslie, quoting his phrase of 1812, 'I have now a path marked out very distinctly for myself', comments that the apparent indecisiveness of the artist's character concealed a rigid determination to excel and a clear knowledge of the line he intended to pursue. At the time of his marriage the course of study of which he had spoken to Benjamin West was, he felt, complete; he now wanted to set to work on paintings which clamoured to be noticed and proclaimed his talents unmistakably. To this end he intended to paint on a relatively large scale. The size he chose for these affirmations of his power was in the main 'a six-foot canvas'; that is, one measuring 6 × 4½ ft.

To construct these important works, which will be studied in some detail in this chapter, he adopted a fairly rigorous routine. He started his preparations in the autumn for the exhibition which would open in the following May. Frequently these preparations included making a full-scale sketch; in any case they involved full recourse to the vocabulary of oil sketches and drawings described in the preceding chapters.

There has inevitably been much discussion of the relative merits of the sketches, large and small, and the carefully worked out, unspontaneous, exhibited pictures. And indeed there is a curious dichotomy between the Constable of the open-air sketches, painting in a whirlwind of inspiration, and the architect of the deliberate works whose construction and handling took many months of work in his studio. In the former the initial art of conception was also the conclusion; over the latter the artist found it difficult ever to convince himself that he had finished his picture. But before the merits of the two types of painting can be judged it is necessary to take a detailed look at the half-dozen or so works on which he himself based his claim to artistic immortality.

The insight for which his long series of brilliant sketches was only a prelude was re-embodied, most deliberately, in a series of six large scenes of the canalized River Stour; these he exhibited between 1819 and 1825. The subjects were all places within a three-mile radius, in a short walking distance from East Bergholt, and all include an event from the canal's life as well as a particularization of the weather which gives each scene its predominant tone.

The precise significance of the theme of a painting was a source of recondite importance throughout the nineteenth century; this is well shown by the strange circumstance that Frith was unable to make a painting of 'Whiteley's at Four o'clock in the Afternoon' or 'The Trial of the Tichborne Claimant' because he could not find in these subjects one main incident of dramatic force. While Constable made no such extravagant demands upon his material, he could not settle down to painting a transcription of his favourite landscape without fixing upon an episode which contributed a narrative note; for instance, the closing of lock-gates, or the leaping of a tow-horse over a barrier in its path.

This fascinating series of scenes, which is so central to Constable's art, had an unobtrusive prelude in his *Flatford Mill* of 1812, *The Mill Stream* of 1814, and *Boatbuilding near Flatford Mill* of 1815. The first-named, now only known from a reproduction of nearly forty years ago, depends fairly literally upon the sketch; it resembles this study rounded off and made complete, but without dramatic changes in intention. *The Mill Stream*, now at Ipswich, is a view which includes Willy Lott's house from a viewpoint near that of *The Hay Wain*, and takes its title from the ferry boat which carried the farmers to their fields on the other bank. Constable lavished a great deal of care on the picture, retaining breadth without sacrificing the natural effect, but the scale was too small for him to remain content with it as the full expression of his ambitions.

The main painting of the Stour exhibited in the next year, 1815, *Boatbuilding near Flatford Mill*, is somewhat anomalous at this particular moment in Constable's career, revealing something of a backward glance. It has been asserted, on Leslie's unimpeachable authority, that it was painted entirely in the open air. What makes this fact so strange is that while engaged upon the painting Constable made in his small 1814 sketch-book an elaborate and, for its size, fully detailed pencil drawing for the composition. The picture follows this small full-page sketch with great literalness, though some of the figures and the details of tools and lumber in the barge-builder's field are taken from sketches on adjacent pages of the book.

The reason for the temporary atavism of this work is to be found in the kindly meant pressure of his friends and his family. Farington urged him to look at Claude before he went for his summer's sketching in the fields; his uncle, David Pike Watts, besought him to give a higher finish to his works, and even his father (no art critic) had suggested that he should 'think less and finish as you go (perhaps that may do)'. And so Constable worked away day after day in the fields during the summer of 1814, staying until he saw the smoke of the workmen's supper fire rising in the evening air, and making a Claude out of the manufacture of another barge for the Stour traffic. The scene was again a family one; the small sunken dry dock in which the barges were built was on his father's land as part of the property of Flatford Mill. The barge, which was destined to transport his father's corn, would, when completed, be floated out on to the main stream of the Stour, just above the lock, which is barely visible on the left of the painting. Leslie, always a perceptive and sympathetic judge of his friend's work, esteemed this picture most highly as a representation of a hot summer's day. He pointed out that hot colours are absent, and indeed the normal blue of the sky is hazed to grey and the ground is golden in tone. Yet there is an element of effort in the result which does not occur in later work. So far as we know, Constable did not attempt to paint again so painstakingly in the open air; his future Stour scenes were larger and were painted in his studio.

Even so, he worked only gradually up to his largest scale. The *Flatford Mill on the River Stour* of 1817, now in the Tate Gallery, which really anticipates his series of large canal scenes, is only 4 ft 2 in. wide, as against the 6 ft of such successors as *The White Horse* and *The Hay Wain*. None the less the painting deserves careful consideration, both because it was his most ambitious work at the time of its exhibition and because it was the first-fruit of the new determination to excel induced by his marriage. Constable's early name for the picture seems to have been 'Flatford Mill, Horse and Barge', though he exhibited it as 'Scene on a navigable river'.

The work was well advanced when Farington saw it in January 1817 and described it in his diary as 'a large landscape, composed of the Scenery about Dedham in Essex'. It represents the River Stour as the canalized highway for the corn ground at his father's mill. Two barges are being manoeuvred on the short reach between Flatford Lock and Flatford Bridge; the first timbers of the footbridge appear in the left-hand bottom corner of the painting. A boy is disconnecting the rope by which they were attached to the tow-horse, and a man with a pole is working on the leading barge, running it into position. The operation is presumably necessary to bring the barges to the other side of the bridge, after which they were to be reconnected to the horse; its leisurely nature is expressed by the nonchalant interest being taken by the boy on horseback and by the figure lying on the second barge. In the middle distance are the red-brick buildings of Flatford Mill, where the artist's father had actually lived till within two years of John Constable's birth. The lock at the mill is the right-hand arm of a fork of water which goes round an island. The two very recognizable trees in the right foreground were often

drawn by Constable, and comparison between his drawings shows the care with which he studied the growth and
decay of the natural objects which he knew so intimately.
Drawings in the sketch-books of 1813 and 1814 show
clearly that the left-hand member of the foremost tree
divided into two limbs, giving it three main stems in all.
Both in the paintings and in a later drawing of the same
year the middle member is no longer to be seen, its position
being marked by a bulbous growth from which it had fallen
or been cut. This is a good example of the particularization,
the concern with individual form, which Constable opposed
to the generalization, the abstraction towards an ideal tree,
of eighteenth-century theory.

In common with the scenes to which it forms a prelude
the subject-matter is an amalgam of familiar, homely,
workaday actions, viewed under a characteristic summer
sky. In this painting the sky is marked by two or three lines
of low, fine-weather cumulus clouds, grey underneath, and
with large patches of blue through which the sun shines to
irradiate the meadows on the right. Here the hay has just
been cut and stacked; a solitary man with a scythe is seen
walking off the field on the completion of his task. The only
other occupants of the scene who are not involved either
in the transit of barges or the reaping of the hay are the
two boys fishing from the middle of the towpath.

The viewpoint has been chosen in such a way as to give
a steeply converging perspective and to intensify the sense
of distance between the spectator and the background of
the view. This is so frequently a facet of Constable's landscape that we may wonder whether it is an instance of his
reverting to the childish vision he had of the riverside, so
that the painted scene gives an effect of strangeness, comparable with the common experience of returning to a childhood home and finding it much smaller in reality than in
imagination. That this effect does exist is shown by Leslie's
comment on first visiting the Constable country: 'in the
larger compositions, he has increased the width of the river
to great advantage'. But we know that Constable had
dreamed of pictures of these scenes as a boy, and the appar-

ent enlargement of them to which Leslie refers is dependent on his choice of viewpoint rather than on a falsification of his material. In contrast with later members of the series the picture is entirely painted with the brush in a fluid style, without the use of impasto or the palette knife. Constable may have worked up this detailed rendering of a serene summer day in the Stour Valley from sketches made at different dates, but no full-scale study is known. The farthest plane of the picture, containing the mill buildings, has only an identity of subject with the sketch of *c*. 1811 which he worked up into a complete picture; this detail conceivably came from a different unknown oil sketch. The only certain collocation is with a drawing in the 1813 sketch-book, which shows the edge of the bridge, the right-hand trees, and the course of the towpath from almost exactly the same viewpoint. It would be interesting to know why nearly six months after exhibiting the work Constable made a finely detailed but repetitious pencil drawing of the clump of foreground trees, now in the Victoria and Albert Museum. Was he anxious to repaint this passage, or was he preserving a record of it in case the painting was sold? In fact, the work did not sell, either at the Royal Academy or the British Institution, to which he sent it in the following year. It remained in the Constable family's collection until it was bequeathed by Miss Isabel Constable to the National Gallery in 1888.

Two years later Constable surpassed this achievement by exhibiting *The White Horse* at the Academy. The canvas measured over 6 ft 2 in. by 4 ft 3 in. and was the largest he had yet attempted; it remained the norm for his future ambitions, and in this way his series of large canal scenes was at last fully launched. This painting and its five successors were the works on which he purposefully staked his claim on the future. When he wanted to appear at his best at a loan exhibition, whether at the British Institution in London or at the Salon in Paris, and when invited to show in Edinburgh, Worcester or Lille, his mind turned to one of the series, which he would send from his studio or borrow from its owner. *The Hay Wain*, which has become through

its position in the National Collection and the countless re-
productions the most popular embodiment of Constable's
art, occupies a central place as the third in order of production of the series of six large Stour scenes. While the
impact and merits of the individual paintings are well
understood, their importance as a group, as a successive and
progressive exploration of a particular *idée fixe*, is perhaps
less well appreciated, because the accidents of time have
dispersed them, and it may never be possible to bring them
together in one place at the same time. Two, *The White
Horse* and the *View on the Stour* are in American collections whose regulations do not admit of loans; two, *Stratford Mill* and *The Lock*, are in private collections in England; *The Leaping Horse* is in the Royal Academy, and is
better known through the full-scale sketch for it in the Victoria and Albert Museum; *The Hay Wain* is alone well
known to the gallery-goer in its final, exhibited form.

The White Horse shows a small reach of the Stour
between Flatford and Dedham, where the towpath switches
from one bank of the river to the other, to avoid crossing
a number of small tributary streams. At this point, since
there was no convenient bridge, it was the bargemen's custom to ferry the tow-horse on one of the barges over to the
other bank, and it is this action which Constable has chosen
as the narrative incident of his painting. The white horse
which gives the picture its name stands in the stern of the
barge approaching the landing-stage on the nearer bank,
from which he will continue the haul towards Flatford. On
the farther bank is a group of farm buildings amidst trees;
beyond them on the right is a view up to the slopes of East
Bergholt.

Constable rarely expended much care in the titles of his
paintings when he first exhibited them, and he simply called
this 'A scene on the River Stour' for the catalogue of the
1819 exhibition; he sometimes referred to it as 'The Farmyard', but its customary and more distinctive title, *The
White Horse*, is apparently due to John Fisher. The sky is
again composed of light fair-weather cloud, with blue at the
zenith; Constable described the scene as 'a placid repre-

sentation of a serene grey morning, summer'. It may be noted that 'placid' was one of his favourite terms of praise; he refers somewhere to his wife as 'my placid and contented companion'.

So far as is known it was during the composition of this picture that Constable first made a full-scale sketch before starting on the version he intended to exhibit; a practice he repeated for a number of others. The sketch, which is now in the National Gallery, Washington, is not as dashing as the final version, since it was painted on a dark ground which now shows through and dulls the thin pigment. When the final version was returned to his studio after exhibition at the Royal Academy, Constable added some work to it; this is the first recorded instance of a practice which was to become common in his later years, developing almost into a vice. His purpose in this instance was to subdue the lights and cool the tones; but to judge by the present fresh and ingratiating aspect of the original he did not carry this process to excessive lengths.

In the construction of the picture he turned, as he had for *Flatford Mill*, and as he would again, to his small and crowded sketch-books of 1813 and 1814. From them he took a study of the whole central area of the farm on the farther bank, including the thatched boat shed, and also two details of the foreground, the posts of the landing-stage and the reeds and water-lilies (this last motif he used again in *Stratford Mill* and *View on the Stour*).

The White Horse proved to Constable that he could paint an evocation of the Suffolk countryside on a large scale and with the full amount of lush, recognizable, emotionally charged detail. It had another important effect, for its reception at the Academy was far warmer than for his earlier exhibits, and some critics even gave Turner second place this year in face of the challenge presented by this picture. The notice taken of it by the public led directly to his long-postponed election as A.R.A. in November 1819, although in the immediately preceding votes his support had been declining. Furthermore, and quite independently of this train of events, his friend John Fisher bought the painting, and installed it in his home at Salisbury. Both the official recognition and the private sale were vitally important in encouraging Constable. Although Fisher's laudatory comment 'the Royal Academy ... an establishment of this great country and, as such, to be held in great respect' may strike strangely on modern ears, there is no doubt that the sentiment echoes Constable's own thought at the time. That he had not been treated with undue kindness by his fellow artists is shown by the fact that William Collins, his junior by twelve years and by far his inferior in capacity, had been an A.R.A. for five years when Constable was elected, and became R.A. the next year, nine years before Constable was successful in attaining that stature. But the whole sequence of events in 1819 justifies Leslie in describing *The White Horse* as on many accounts the most important picture he had painted. To its owner, Fisher, Constable wrote that it was the strongest example in his work of pictures he had thought of as a child.

For the next exhibition, that of 1820, he set out on a more open and less frontally conceived scene of the same size. For the place to be represented he chose the bend of the river flanked on the left by Stratford Mill. This was the farthest point up the river painted by him on a large scale, though even so it is only just over two miles in a direct line from Flatford Lock. Indeed, other studies by him of the river at this point are scarcely known.

Stratford Mill is, however, one of the ramshackle shed-like structures that Constable delighted in, and it stood on an island guarded by rotting water-immersed stumps. The mill building and the barge anchored to the farther bank constitute the main references in his picture to the canal's normal working function, but the chief incident is provided by the group of four boys fishing in the foreground. When Lucas published his mezzotint of the painting, after Constable's death, he called it 'The Young Waltonians' in reference to this episode; it is fairly certain that the painter would have disapproved of so overt a reference to this particular feature. Even so, the illustration of fishing in the picture led to its inclusion for a time in the National

Gallery of British Sports and Pastimes formed by Mr Walter Hutchinson.

There is a shower passing in the distance, but the exquisitely managed reflection of the trees in the foreground sets the mood of summer serenity which is the keynot of this painting as much as of its predecessor, *The White Horse*. Studies for the detail are rare, but for the water-lilies in the foreground Constable again made use of his 1813 sketch-book. Once more, when the painting was returned to his studio after the exhibition Constable carried out some further work upon it.

As in the year before, Fisher bought this most important work, not for his own collection but as a present to a Salisbury solicitor, J. P. Tinney, who had won a lawsuit for him. This generous action, though it was a gratification to Constable when it was made, had an unfortunate sequel. Tinney, with considerable good nature, having heard that Constable was not selling as many pictures as he would wish, offered to buy his next large piece if it remained unsold after exhibition; at the same time he commissioned two large upright canvases, leaving the choice of subjects to Constable. The very flexibility and reasonableness of this arrangement made it irksome to the beneficiary. Constable delayed and delayed until a flood of orders from Paris dealers made the execution of the scheme a psychological impossibility. In the meantime he behaved as though *Stratford Mill*, Fisher's gift to Tinney, was still his own property; he summoned it back to his studio, painted upon it, sent it to exhibitions without much consideration for the owner. In all these transactions Fisher acted as a patient, good-humoured intermediary. Ultimately Constable begged to be let off Tinney's commissions, at the expense of a row with him and Fisher. Although his behaviour in the transaction was unreasonable and can only be condoned by attributing it to a fit of the 'artistic temperament' to which he was not usually prone, Constable did at least demonstrate by it the sincerity of his conviction that *Stratford Mill* was his most important work. He described it as 'grander' than its successor *The Hay Wain*, and it was the piece he most wished to represent him in loan exhibitions.

At this point there might have come a break in the series of Stour Valley scenes, for Constable was beginning to work up into a large-scale form his ideas for a Thames landscape on the theme of the opening of Waterloo Bridge. He intended to make this his chief exhibit at the Royal Academy exhibition of 1821, but Joseph Farington strongly advised him to continue his series of Suffolk subjects. Accordingly, in November 1820, rather late for the next year's exhibition, he roughed out the full-size oil sketch for *The Hay Wain*, and then proceeded with the more finished exhibition piece, continuing his practice by working on it further after the show had closed.

In this picture he turned to the most familiar sketching-ground of all – the path in front of Flatford Mill, his father's first home, where his elder sister and brother were born. To these associations were attached in Constable's tenacious memory the story of Willy Lott's house, the cottage-farmhouse which is prominent in the picture. The farmer, Willy Lott, was alive in Constable's own time, and in the eighty years of his life spent only four days away from his home. This classic example of Suffolk obstinacy was precisely the behaviour to appeal to Constable's sense of continuity and tradition, and added an associative value to the house.

The scene is a half-open one, closed in at the left by the buildings and spreading out over the meadows on the right; thus it is less hemmed in than *The White Horse*, but rather less open than *Stratford Mill*. It was partly for this reason that Constable thought that *Stratford Mill* was the more imposing painting, though he thought he had given *The Hay Wain* a novel look.

The title Constable gave the painting for the exhibition was simply 'Landscape: Noon'; it is interesting that though he specifies neither the place nor the season he is precise about the time of day, which accounts for the vertical light illuminating the structure of the trees. The growth and colour of the trees, and the hay in the wain, show that the picture represents an early summer day; there are high, fair-weather clouds, and the scanty drift of smoke from the farmhouse chimney indicates only a light breeze. The animation of the scene, no less than its title, is provided by the cart crossing the ford. The painting is unique among the six grand landscapes in having no barge, but it appears from a small rough sketch of the composition, now in the Paul Mellon Collection, that even in this work Constable had intended to introduce a sailing-barge on the main arm of the river canal. If such was his intention, he changed it as he worked the theme up to its fuller scale.

It is a tantalizing question whether, in choosing the theme of a hay cart crossing a ford, Constable had in mind any of the landscapes with this same subject painted by the late seventeenth-century Flemish artist Siberechts. By working in England for a number of years this artist left an impression on the national school and, although Constable did not mention his name in the series of lectures he gave on the history of landscape painting, he clearly admired his work, of which he possessed an example.

Constable had already made a number of oil sketches and drawings from the viewpoint he has chosen here, and possibly for this reason the full-scale oil sketch in the Victoria and Albert Museum is more generalized and less worked out in detail than any other extant example of his large studies. The honey-brown ground, itself distinct from the harsher red with which he usually primed his canvases, acts as a warm middle tint out of which he has picked the highlights of the cottage, the water, and the meadows beyond. Here, beyond the mere masses of the composition, he is mainly concerned to work out the balance of tones, the overall light and shade of the picture. It is so clearly an experimental blocking-out of the masses, on which more work in defining the forms and making the colours more natural is expected, that it is (unlike some of the other sketches) impossible even to conceive of its being exhibited in the generation in which it was painted.

Constable did not make many changes in the composition when he repeated it for the finished work. He painted out the figure on horseback on the nearer bank of the stream (said to represent his father), and modified the drawing of the wain to make it fit with a drawing of a harvest wagon ('scrave' in the local dialect) for which he asked the younger Dunthorne. At the same time he brought all the forms into clearer focus and made them more definite; especially the cottage, to which he added a chimney, and the meadows, trees and ridge in the middle distance. The sky also, so perfectly judged a part of the whole painting, he changed so that it became less overcast and had more sharply defined clouds. A tree which in the sketch looks as though it had been transferred from the right-hand side of *The White Horse* to the middle of *The Hay Wain* has been more sharply differentiated. Here, as in all his studies of Willy Lott's house, Constable pays great attention to the little bush in the angle below the waterside gate, which gives a dusting of sparkling foliage in this shadowy place.

The Hay Wain more than any other of his paintings has come to represent Constable's art in its maturity, and its pre-eminent appeal began soon after its completion. When it was seen at the Royal Academy exhibition of 1821 it was greatly admired by Géricault and by some French critics. Partly as a result of Géricault's enthusiasm it was borrowed for the Paris Salon of 1824 and led to the influential intervention by Constable in the progress of French landscape painting. From this work Delacroix learned a lesson in the management of dramatic contrast, and it was bought from the Salon for a French collection. Its history as part of the landscape of almost every English mind begins with its purchase for the National Gallery in 1886. But to Constable it was simply the third of a series of six large canal scenes, and not especially exceptional among them.

Constable had no doubts about sending another view of the Stour to the Royal Academy in 1822. Already in September 1821 he was 'behindhand' with this project. This year he had fixed upon the short reach between Flatford Lock and Flatford Mill as the scene for his picture – almost exactly a reverse view from that seen in the Tate Gallery's *Flatford Mill*. The lock is not seen, and the viewpoint is

from the other bank, on which there is no towpath. The
distribution of trees and buildings is less closed in than in
The Hay Wain; Constable has reverted to the more open
composition of *Stratford Mill*. The full-scale sketch was
worked out with much care, and it was from the sketch, not
the exhibited painting, that Lucas made his mezzotint 'View
on the Stour near Dedham'. Constable himself described the
changes he made from the composition of the sketch when
painting the finished picture: 'I have taken the sail, and
added another barge in the middle of the picture, with a
principal figure, altered the group of trees, and made the
bridge entire. The picture has now a rich centre, and the
right hand side becomes only an accessory. I have endeavoured to paint with more delicacy, but hardly anyone
has seen it.' This last sentence refers to the criticism, current even in 1822, of his harsh, strongly accented, rough
brushwork.

In its final form the *View of the Stour* shows the usual
gang of two barges being manoeuvred by boys; a tow-horse
is on the path beyond them, and on the left is a barge with
its sail half erected. In the distance another barge is seen
rounding a bend in the river, and the tower of Dedham
Church is placed beyond. A girl is crossing the footbridge from the direction of Bridge Cottage: in the sketch
Constable had put only a cow here, but in the mezzotint
which Lucas made, primarily from the sketch, both this
girl and the cow appear. Swallows are skimming the surface
of the water; water-weeds and the rotting posts in which the
painter delighted are seen in the right foreground, where a
fishing-boat is moored and an eel spear lies on the ground.
A blue sky, with soft cumulus clouds, is allied with the
summer light in the picture. However, when he directed
the engraving of the picture Constable introduced a stormier
sky.

In planning both the scene and its detail Constable
turned again to the seminal years of reflection and visual
experiment which he had undertaken in 1813 and 1814.
One of the pages in the 1814 sketch-book shows the middle
and right-hand sections of the composition; even the figure

on the bridge is there, and the point at which the ridge of the cottage roof is cut off on the right is the same. The left-hand section of trees he seems to have made up from two other pages in the same book, whilst the motif of the boy poling the nearer barge is derived from a thumbnail sketch in the 1813 sketch-book.

In four successive years he had sent four six-foot canvases to the Academy. The break in the sequence which he had first thought of making in 1821 did, in fact, occur in 1823. This came about partly because he had impoverished himself by his effort, and had to attend seriously to commissions which would bring in some ready money; partly because he was prevented by ill health from bringing the successor he was planning (*The Lock*) to a sufficient state of readiness. His major exhibit in 1823 was accordingly the *Salisbury Cathedral from the Bishop's Grounds*, now in the Victoria and Albert Museum. This was the outcome of a commission from Dr John Fisher, over which Constable had delayed more than two years; and although the canvas was only a three-foot one he started it so late in the year that he had an agonizing struggle to get it ready for the Academy in the next spring.

Joseph Farington died in 1821, and Constable had moved into his house in Charlotte Street. This was prompted by his need for a better studio, and for more space. 'We are', he wrote of his old home, quoting his favourite Cowper, 'like bottled wasps upon a southern wall.' But in moving from Keppel Street he felt a sentimental pang at leaving a house where he had been so happy and 'where I painted my four landscapes'; the phrase – referring to the four large canal scenes so far discussed in this chapter – shows what a place apart in his work they held for him.

When he resumed the series, in 1824, he introduced a variation by upending the canvas and constructing the scene in a vertical formation; the overall dimensions are also reduced, the height being only 4 ft 8 in. The painting now known as *The Lock* but called by Constable 'A barge shooting a Lock' was his only exhibit this year, and proved to be the most immediately successful of all his canal scenes.

It was sold on the day the exhibition opened to a stranger, Mr Charles Morrison, a descendant of whom still owns it. Furthermore he was called upon to make a number of repetitions of the work; some of these, including the well-known version in the Diploma Gallery at Burlington House, he converted to a horizontal format.

The scene is once again Flatford Lock, looking towards Flatford Bridge. The viewpoint is at the seaward end of the lock, and the level of sight has been adjusted to the lower of the two sheets of water, as though it had been taken from a barge at the lower gate. In the earliest, exhibited version, the angle of vision is concentrated upon the meadows which sweep down to Dedham, and the river's course is not conspicuous. In this way Constable has evolved an entirely novel composition from a viewpoint which is, in fact, very close to that in two other pictures of his, the *A Lock on the Stour* of 1813 and the *View on the Stour near Dedham* of 1822, its immediate predecessor among the canal subjects.

Constable himself thought that he had achieved his intentions in the painting: 'It is silvery, windy, and delicious; all health, and the absence of everything stagnant.' This good opinion was shared by a number of his contemporaries. The engraver, S. W. Reynolds, himself a sensitive landscape painter, wrote him a eulogistic letter comparing it with Wilson and Gainsborough. He offered to engrave it at his own expense, and, although he died before the plate could be completed, this proposal had the important consequence of introducing Constable to Reynolds's apprentice David Lucas, who was to become so closely involved in his fame.

Besides the full-size sketch for the painting (now in the Philadelphia Museum of Art) there are repetitions of *The Lock* which repeat its upright format. One of these was blocked in outline by his studio assistant John Dunthorne, the son of Constable's boyhood sketching comrade. The increasing popularity of his work, calling for repetitions of some specific compositions, had made this sort of help in mechanical parts a necessity. Then, carried away by his delight in the scene and encouraged by its exceptional success, Constable painted some variations in a horizontal format. One of them, painted in 1826, was commissioned by the dealer W. H. Carpenter. An extension of the composition to the right has enabled him to include a distant view of Bridge Cottage and Flatford Bridge, and he has changed the action of the boy at the lock-gate and the position of the barge. So well did he like this version that when he was elected a full Royal Academician in 1829 Constable obtained it from the owner and presented it as his Diploma picture. Perhaps by this time some of the freshness of the first conception had worn away; and, in accord with a development commonly seen in his later years the weather, formerly dominated by a healthy wind, gets rainier and more disturbed. In the mezzotint which Lucas made from the original version Constable worked so much on the sky during the progress of the engraving that it became, in the end, menacing and stormy.

The Leaping Horse, which he prepared for the exhibition of 1825, was destined to be the last of this compact series of canal scenes which lies at the centre of Constable's career, though he did not plan it in any valedictory mood and such a picture as *The Valley Farm* of ten years later should perhaps be regarded as a sequel. In the creation of this great work the ambivalence between the sketch and the exhibited picture developed to its closest extreme, till there was scarcely anything to choose between the two in degree of finish, and Constable himself was chronically uncertain which to send in. But in this case the version which he came to regard solely as the sketch is the more vital and the finer painting.

For his viewpoint Constable has moved back up the river, just passing the scene of his first subject on the grand scale, *The White Horse*. The narrative element was suggested by the practice of training the canal's tow-horses to jump over the barriers erected across the towpath to prevent cattle from straying. This vigorous and impressive sight gives the picture its action and its name. Constable himself described the content of the picture in less specific terms,

singling out the elements which always appealed to him as
a spectator of the life of the riverbank, most of which indeed are common to all his six large paintings:

'It is a canal, and full of the bustle incident to such a
scene where four or five boats are passing with dogs,
horses, boys and men and women and children, and best of
all old timber props, water plants, willow stumps, sedges,
old nets, etc. etc.' Later he described the content of the
painting as 'lively and soothing, calm and exhilarating,
fresh and blowing'.

Since he began to paint the picture only five months
before it was due for exhibition, Constable left himself extremely short of the time he needed for reflection, correc-
tion, and concentration. This atmosphere of hurry probably
accounts for the uncertainties, exceptional even for so self-
critical an artist, which he felt about the final form of the
composition, and about which of the two versions of his
canal he should regard as the sketch. These indecisions
came to a head over the gnarled tree-stumps to left and
right of the leaping horse. In the exhibited version we now
see only the left-hand one; in the sketch only the one on
the right, but it seems likely that his original intention was
to include both these stumps, and there are, in fact, signs on
both canvases of the former presence of two. When he sent
the picture to the Royal Academy it still had both trees in
it; and he only painted out the right-hand one in this
version after it had returned, unsold, to his studio.

The viewpoint of the painting is almost as low as that
used in *The Lock*, placing the line of vision below the
level of the towpath itself. The two barges which are being
towed by the leaping horse are in the left foreground of the
painting, the foremost one, or cabin boat, being distinguished by the blue smoke rising from its galley. Other
barges are beating back into the scene on a more distant
reach of the river. The exhibited version originally followed the sketch even more closely than it does now, and
shows by its *pentimenti* the extent of Constable's changes of
mind. For instance, he painted out the barge on the extreme
left and the cow coming down to the river to drink, at the

same time altering the contour of the remaining barge to give a less head-on view. To this barge he added a half-furled sail, and in order to provide a distant landmark he painted in the tower of Dedham Church, which, it may be surmised, is not really visible at this point.

The sketch is more successful than the exhibited painting because it suffered less from his later and often more timid after-thoughts and remained the homogeneous expression of his first intentions. No feature in it is emphasized at the expense of others, and the basis of its execution is the palette knife, which at the time Constable was using to produce effects of great breadth and violent transitions of tone, at the same time enlivening the surface as in a mosaic by varying the angle at which the paint takes the light. In the exhibited version, now at Burlington House, Constable began with a similarly broad painting, but he worked some passages – the horse and the boy on its back, the sky, the surface of the river – to a higher degree of finish, and the inconsistency between the two methods of approach gives a discordant effect to the whole. None the less, it was in *The Leaping Horse* that Constable reached the climax, both pictorial and emotional, of the sequence of canal scenes. The bold, agitated handling matches the more tempestuous sky with its broken lights and is underlined by the leading symbol in the picture, that of the horse gathering itself for its strong jump over the barrier. This is the most violent gesture in his paintings, anticipated to some degree by the action of the lock-keeper in *The Lock*, the immediate precursor of *The Leaping Horse*.

As we look back over the six large canal scenes, now terminated by *The Leaping Horse*, it can be seen that they conform to a general pattern into which the artist has introduced a progressive development. To begin with the elements of their construction, they all have the horizon about two-fifths of the way up the picture; this has the effect of bringing the lines of convergence of the picture's perspective to the eye-level of a six-foot man if the painting should be hung on the 'line' at the Royal Academy. After the detailed descriptions which have been given it is unnecessary to stress further the complete homogeneity of subject-matter. This was the very point on which Constable had been quizzed by Fisher: 'I hope you will a little diversify your subject this year as to time of day. Thomson, you know, wrote not four Summers, but four Seasons. People are tired of mutton on top, mutton at bottom, mutton at the side dishes, though of the best flavour and smallest size.' To this Constable replied in self-justification – it was while he was planning *The Leaping Horse* – 'I do not enter into that notion of varying one's plans to keep the publick in good humour. Subject and change of weather and effect will afford variety in landscape.' He goes on to say: 'I imagine myself driving a nail; I have driven it some way – by persevering with this nail I may drive it home ... No man who can do any one thing well, will ever be able to do another different as well; I believe that from our physical construction no man can be born with more than one high and original feel. This in my opinion was the case with the greatest master of variety – Shakespeare.'

Whilst *The White Horse* and *The Hay Wain* are enclosed views, with large massed trees filling the canvas on the left, the remainder are more open towards the sky. As he approached the end of the series the serene summer weather playing over the Stour becomes more overcast. This tendency, noticeable even in the first version of *The Lock*, becomes more apparent in *The Leaping Horse*. The mezzotints which Lucas made in the 1830s from the paintings were all given, under the painter's guidance, stormier skies than the originals. Though the process had begun earlier, this progressive leaning towards the dramatic and morbidly romantic was no doubt a reflex of his growing personal troubles in the death of his wife, the care of his family, and the partial exhaustion of his invention.

The seven years during which Constable planned, painted, and exhibited these paintings were the most productive of his life, and mark that stage of his career when his art was most mature and when he was brimming over with new ideas. This enhanced creativity is seen in his increasing boldness of brushwork and knife-work and in the inventiveness with which he gives animation and light to his paint surface. *The White Horse* and *Stratford Mill* are comparatively smooth in handling, but by the time he came to paint *The Hay Wain* he was able to achieve, by the full use of impasto, the broken, crumbling effect of his most developed manner. Therefore it was peculiarly fortunate that this was the painting chosen to represent him in the Paris Salon of 1824, where it caused the spectators to say: 'Look at these English pictures – the very dew is on the ground.' The characteristics in *The Hay Wain* which Constable himself described as richness of texture and attention to the surface of objects were the qualities which so impressed Delacroix and led to one of the best-attested and most remarkable contacts between English and French art. His method of rendering the richness of light by juxtaposing dots of colour reaches its apogee in *The Leaping Horse*, where he achieves these results with the palette knife and bold flat masses of undiluted colour. The six canal scenes in which he embodied these rich and novel resources and on which he expended such intense thought and inflexible will-power amount in their entirety to Constable's appropriation and exaltation of his own countryside.

5

THE EXTENDED VISTA

THE large Suffolk paintings which are the subject of the preceding chapter were the works to which Constable attached
most importance; but the landscape of the Stour was, of
course, not his only theme, nor were the preparations for
the canal pictures his only activities in these years. The
course of his life is shot through with the paradox that,
although he considered subject-matter to be of minor importance, he could not paint a place unless he had deep
personal feelings associated with it.

Leaving on one side his migrations as a student in the
centre of London – which provided him eventually with
one subject, the opening of Waterloo Bridge – the first move
towards a landscape which might share part of the affection
he felt for Suffolk came, as already recounted, when he
visited Salisbury in 1811 and there met John Fisher, who
was to become his lifelong friend. Very soon Salisbury had
become a place with sufficient vivid associations to provide
him with an interest in its landscape and a desire to make
paintings of it; while the immediate result was the calm
painting of *Salisbury: Morning* shown at the Academy in
1812, his more sustained efforts (based upon several drawings and sketches of the Cathedral), culminated in the
Bishop's picture of 1823.

Maria Bicknell's health was delicate even before her
marriage. Soon after the birth of their second child the
inherent weakness – her sister was consumptive – became
more apparent, and in 1819 John Constable took a house in
Hampstead for the later summer months in search of purer
air. This move, taken for reasons of health which soon
became more pressing, unexpectedly extended the scope of
his subject-matter. To the practical advantages of the gravel
soil and the 400-ft elevation above the smoke of London
were added a multitude of scenes which became of associ-

ative interest. In this first visit he made some oil sketches, and kept a small sketch-book in which a number of themes that were later to become dominant already appear. Gradually he forged links of affection and personal regard which enabled him to make from this unspectacular, slightly hilly, semi-urban landscape some of his most considered and popular paintings.

In seeking for equivalents which might link on to his long-forged connections with Suffolk, Constable soon found familiar motifs on Hampstead Heath. The most direct analogy was the sand-pit near Branch Hill Pond, where the day-to-day activity of filling the carts reminded him immediately of the gravel pits on the slopes about Dedham Vale which he had sketched with particular concentration in his 1814 sketch-book and had made a principal feature of Philadelphia Godfrey's wedding present *Stour Valley and Dedham Village*. The horses and carts which plied to and from this pit were frequently the subject of his drawings, and were introduced by him as staffage in such elaborated paintings as *Hampstead Heath: Branch Hill Pond*. Here, too, he found donkeys, an animal which he always delighted in, and which are still used at fairs and for children's rides on the Heath. There was no river to give him flowing water as a foreground, but he frequently used the Branch Hill Pond with its bevy of children bathing as a substitute for this feature. For the views from the ridges of East Bergholt into the valley of the Stour he found some analogy in the wider sweeps over to the north of London; and rather later in his stay at Hampstead found that the view into the Thames Valley was another analogue, the source of remarkable scenic effects and marked by its own vertical feature, the dome of St Paul's Cathedral.

Having made sketches of many of these subjects he began to compose highly-studied paintings from them. Among the first are probably to be included *Upper Heath* in the Fitzwilliam Museum, Cambridge, and the *Hampstead Heath: Vale of Health* in the Victoria and Albert Museum. These may have been painted as companion pieces and seem to be of the same date as the National Gallery's *Salt Box*,

which takes its name from a house on the Heath and is
said by Leslie to have been produced about 1820. Both
have a remarkable serenity of atmosphere, and the handling
reflects the smooth uncomplicated brushwork of his earlier
Suffolk scenes rather than the more complex texture which
he developed in *The Hay Wain*.

The migration to Hampstead became a yearly habit and
eventually he took the house in Well Walk which remained
his property till his death in 1837. During these years his
conception of the scenery of Hampstead, though diversified
into many different subjects, became most concentrated
upon three special themes. Two of them were compositions
showing Branch Hill Pond from the ridge of Judge's Walk,
from near-by viewpoints but with widely different effects.
The most elaborate of these views is best known from a
version formerly in the collection of Sir Joseph Beecham
and now in the collection of Dr Oskar Reinhart. The pond
in this case seems almost on the same level as the spectator;
a half-worked bank of sand fills much of the foreground;
the large house, the Salt Box, is on the right; and an extensive view stretches northward. Constable's own description
to a prospective buyer was 'A scene on Hampstead Heath,
with broken foreground and sand carts, Windsor Castle in
the extreme distance on the right of the shower. The fresh
greens in the distance (which you are pleased to admire)
are the fields about Harrow, and the villages of Hendon,
Kilburn, etc.' The second composition is known from the
version in the Victoria and Albert Museum, from numerous
replicas, and from a number of forgeries. In it the right-
hand feature is more of a hummock than a flat-topped ridge,
and the pond looks lower than in the other. This composition was based upon one of the very first oil sketches he
made at Hampstead in the autumn of 1819. His willingness
to make a number of replicas shows that he did not lose his
enthusiasm for the subject throughout his life.

Besides these two basic scenes there is a third view of
Hampstead which he devised as a companion piece to the
first composition described above. Like its pendant, it shows
a flattish scene without any marked hilly effect in the fore-

ground; a road curves into the foreground from the extensive plain of the middle distance. Constable's description is 'Likewise a scene on Hampstead Heath, called Child's Hill. Harrow with its spire in the distance. Serene afternoon, with sunshine after rain, and heavy clouds passing off. Harvest-time, the foreground filled with cattle and figures, and an Essex market cart.' This description shows that the subject-matter to Constable was as much the season and the weather as the view before him. In fact, when he painted later versions of these patterns, such as *Hampstead Heath: Branch Hill Pond*, he generally took care to vary the atmospheric effect, even to the extent of introducing a rainbow.

The practice of painting variations of his finished pictures has already been encountered with the repetitions of his 1824 painting of *The Lock*. But he had begun to do this at least four years earlier, with versions of the *Dedham Mill*, which was first painted around 1820 and then repeated, with larger or smaller differences, over a number of years. It may seem at first sight surprising that Constable, to whom the actual completion of any composition was a task of such anxiety, should, once he had achieved what he regarded as finality, have been willing to make copies of his own pictures. Yet there are undeniably many authentic replicas, not only of *Dedham Mill*, *Hampstead Heath: Branch Hill Pond*, and *The Lock*, but also of *Salisbury Cathedral from the Bishop's Grounds, The Glebe Farm* and *Summer morning: Dedham from Langham*. The stimulus for these repetitions was generally a private commission, and it is a sign of his growing popularity in the 1820s that he was from this time onwards frequently asked to repeat a specific work. Other replicas were required by his dealers in Paris for exhibition and sale. He had less hesitation in complying with these demands because he was himself an inveterate and excellent copyist of the Old Masters; there was as much competition for his copies of Claude and Poussin as for his own original pieces at the sale after the artist's death. And, with the exception of *The Lock*, the compositions he was called upon to repeat were of a

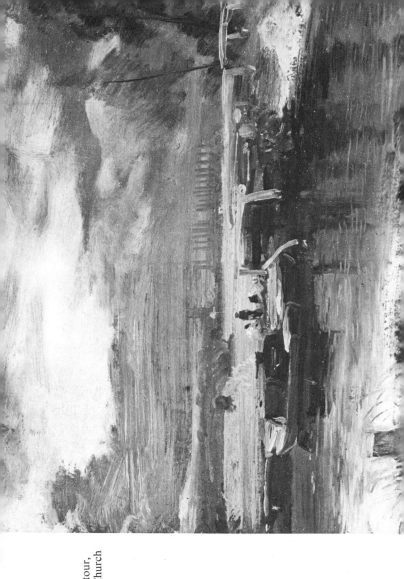

Barges on the Stour,
with Dedham Church
in the distance,
c. 1811

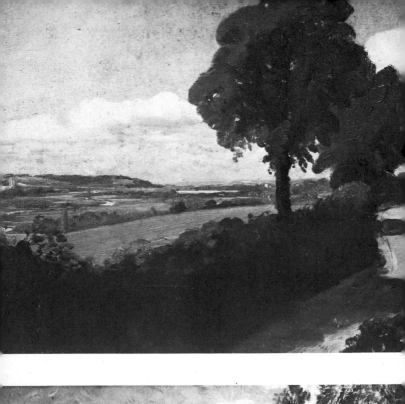

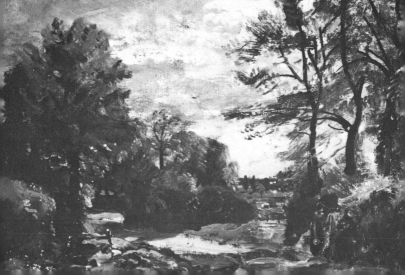

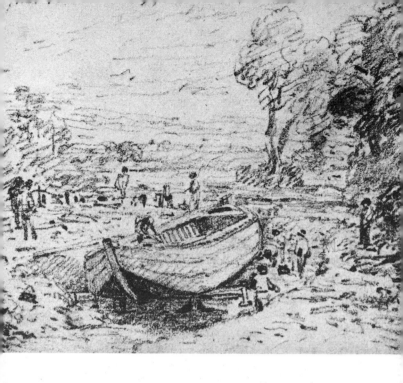

Study for 'Boat-building near
Flatford Mill', 1814

Left above View of Dedham Vale,
c. 1809–14

Left below A country lane near Flatford,
c. 1809–14

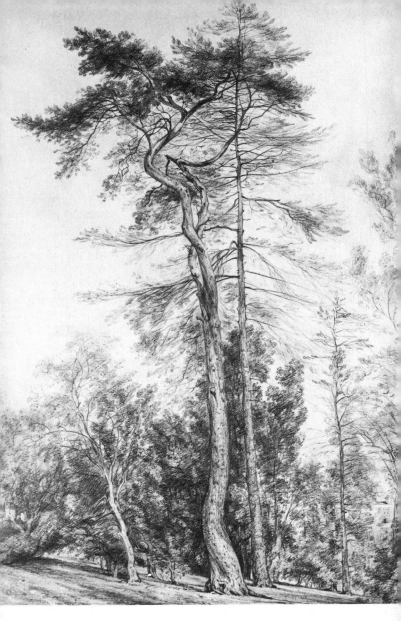

Fir Trees, 1815

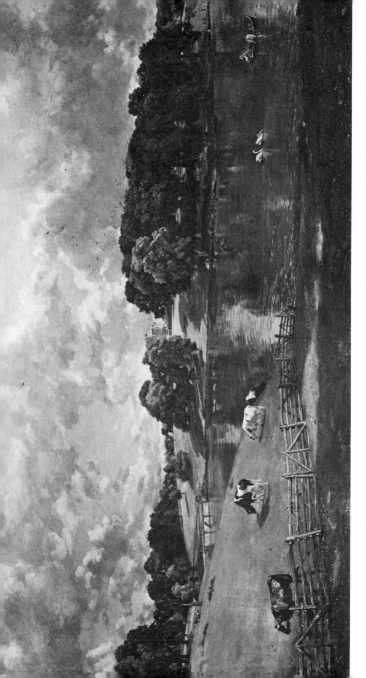

Wivenhoe Park, Essex, 1817 (*Widener Collection*)

Boat-building near
Flatford Mill, 1815

Below The Hay Wain,
1821

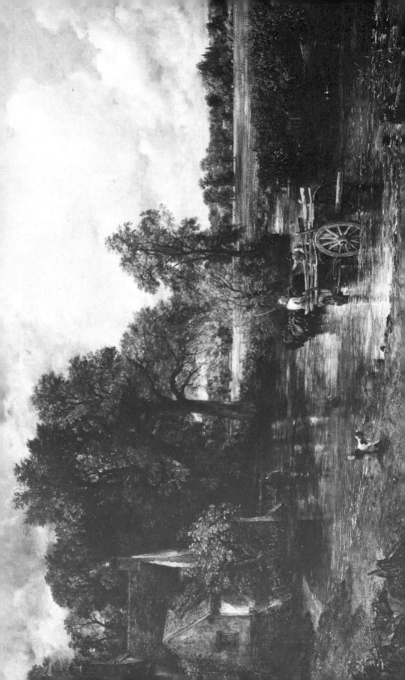

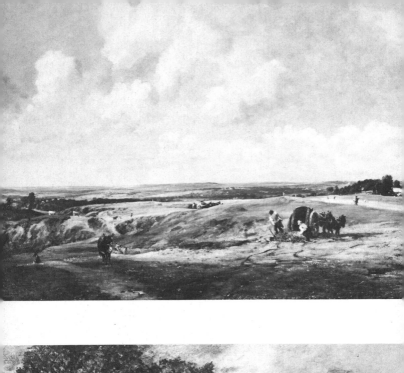

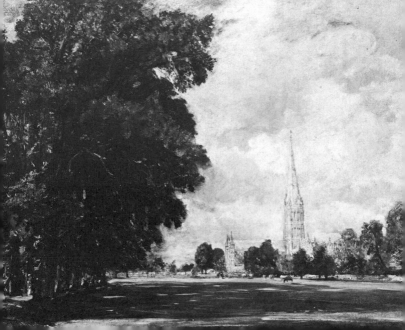

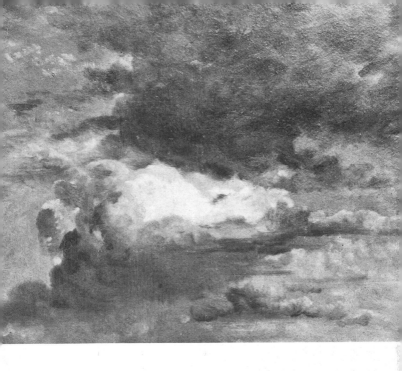

Cloud study, 1822

Opposite above Upper Heath, Hampstead,
near the sand-pits, *c.* 1820

Below A view of Salisbury Cathedral,
c. 1820–2 (*Andrew Mellon Collection*)

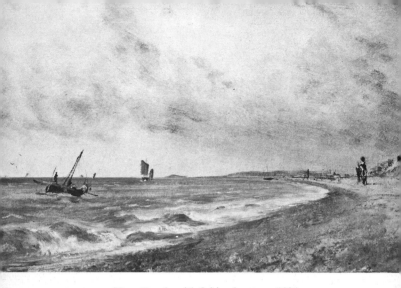

Hove Beach, with fishing boats, *c.* 1824

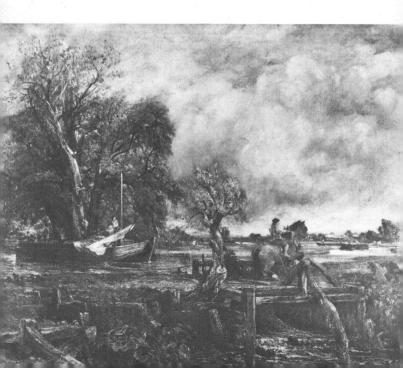

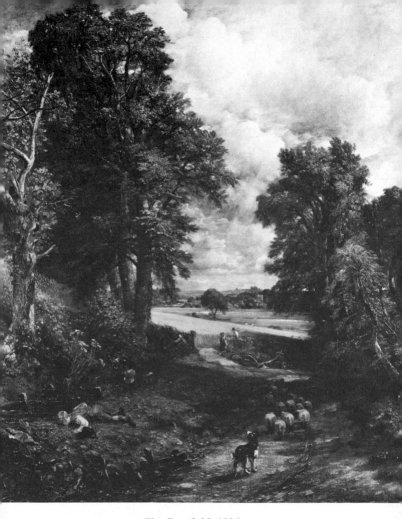

The Cornfield, 1826

Left The Leaping Horse, 1825

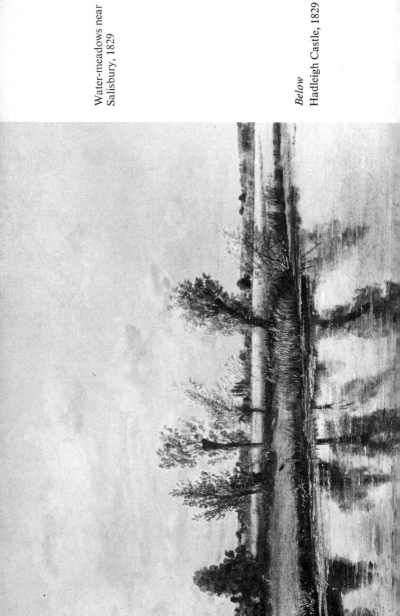

Water-meadows near
Salisbury, 1829

Below
Hadleigh Castle, 1829

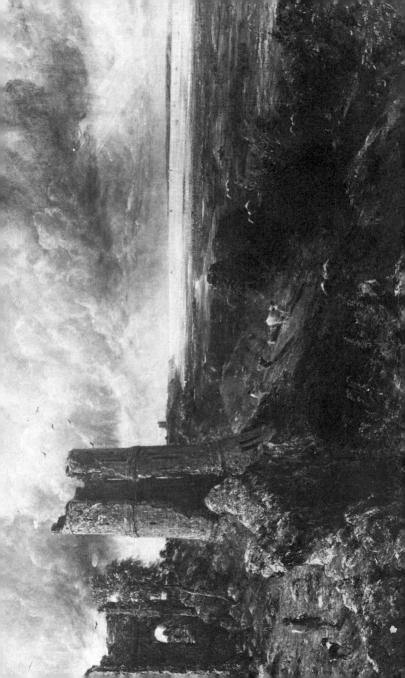

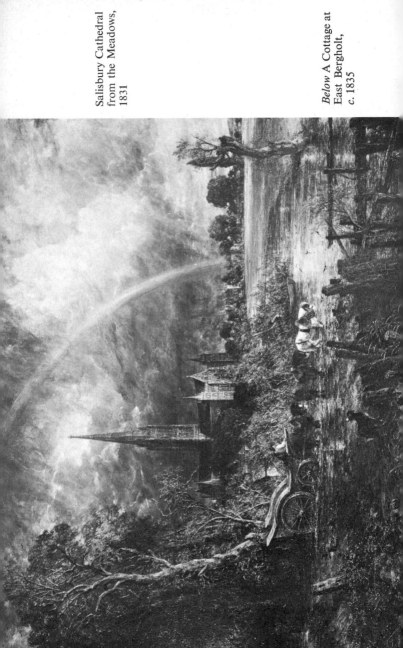

Salisbury Cathedral from the Meadows, 1831

Below A Cottage at East Bergholt, *c.* 1835

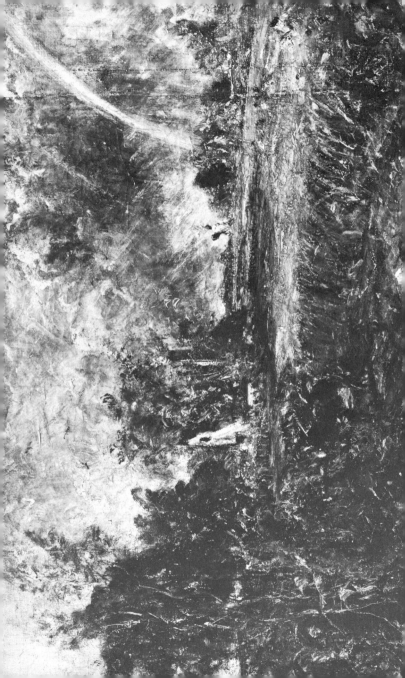

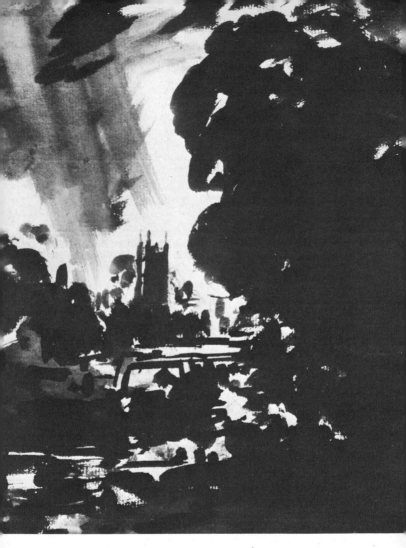

View on the Stour; Dedham Church in the Distance, after 1830

middle or small size, more convenient for his would-be patrons than the great six-footers which Fisher and Tinney had in their homes. For the period when John Dunthorne, junior, was acting as his studio assistant he was employed on copying the outlines of such pieces as the *Salisbury Cathedral from the Bishop's Grounds* for Constable to work up. This is one reason why the replicas rarely have the liveliness of the first authentic versions. And it must be admitted that the alterations which he himself introduced were not always happy in taste. In some of the later versions of *Hampstead Heath: Branch Hill Pond* he replaced the house on the bank by a windmill and added a rainbow to the atmospheric effects, but only succeeded in making the changes look inappropriate.

Although he confined his canvases of Hampstead in the main to the three scenes already described, he made some individual pictures which were not repeated. Two of them, the pendants in the Fitzwilliam and the Victoria and Albert Museum, have been mentioned; another is the upright *Trees near Hampstead Church*, also in the Victoria and Albert Museum, which goes farther than any other oil-painting of his in the literal transcription of individual tree-forms, and is in this aspect comparable with his most meticulous drawings.

Besides these more concentrated efforts Constable was constantly engaged in sketching the neighbourhood of Hampstead. The pattern of his life had changed since his marriage. As before, he spent the winters in the centre of London, first in Keppel Street and later in his house in Charlotte Street. It was in these studios he painted his Academy exhibits, notably his Stour pictures. But he did not now go regularly every summer to East Bergholt: and he came to regard Hampstead as the nearest equivalent to a country outlet from London, a place where he could gain some contact with the wildness of Nature, and where at the same time the health of his wife and children might benefit. He reckoned he was three miles from his painting-rooms in Charlotte Street and that a message would reach him in an hour. The time and creative energy he had spent

C.—D

sketching at East Bergholt and on the Stour he now devoted to Hampstead and its neighbouring villages, Muswell Hill, Child's Hill, Harrow, Highgate. Some of his most unusual and unexpected originalities came out of this activity, including a large number of the drawings, scenes over the Thames valley to St Paul's.

However, the most significant sketches which he made at Hampstead were his famous sky studies. Even here we have to distinguish between two kinds of study in this deliberate exercise. A large group, started in 1821, is characterized by the foregrounds of wind-swept trees, above which is a carefully observed emphatic sky. In the following year he began on a series of pure cloud studies, in which there is no trace at all of the ground below them. Long before he embarked upon this sustained analysis of their transient appearances the clouds in Constable's paintings had been prominent and fitting; there is no clash of subtlety, or lack of appropriateness, in the skies of *Flatford Mill* or *The White Horse*. Why, then, did he throw himself with ever-greater determination into the task of making himself adept in observing the changing form of skies?

There were a number of motives behind his decision. When he moved to Hampstead for his summers he must have found that the most immediate link between the natural scene in East Anglia which he had for a time forsaken and that of North London was to be found in their skies. At the same time he had been thinking deeply about the basis of his art, and had come to realize the great importance of the sky in the total effect of a landscape as he conceived it. This importance is fully recognized in the contemporary craft of landscape photography. To take a homely instance near at hand, we can understand the point at issue by comparing the plates intwo treatises recently issued as paper-backs; those in Professor L. Dudley Stamp's BRITAIN'S STRUCTURE AND SCENERY with those in Professor Gordon Manley's CLIMATE AND THE BRITISH SCENE. Both sets of reproduction have naturally been selected to illuminate the subjects of which the books treat. In the former they exhibit brilliantly the structure of the ground and its rock formations, but there has been no attempt to capture an interesting or characteristic sky above the ground formations. In the book on climate the skies are the leading subject, but the lands which the diversified cloudscapes illuminate are selected with a subtle understanding. The result is that the photographs in the second book completely evoke a characteristic mood of the scenery, whether it be summer over the Skye mountains or December on the Sussex coast.

This is achieved by isolating a quality deeper than the correspondence of form between the sky and the earth; it comes from capturing a consistency between the lighting of the earth and the structure of the light-source in the sky. It might seem absurd to reduce this principle to the statement that a tree should not throw its shadow to the left if the sun is shown in the left-hand corner of the picture; yet nineteenth-century imitations of Guardi used to be distinguished from genuine works by the neglect of just this principle. In the more sensitive terms in which Constable defined it, the basic fact is that any specific effect of lighting on the ground is consistent with one, and only one, distribution of clouds and with one position of the sun in the sky. At the time when he was fully engaged in his sky studies he wrote a letter to John Fisher, now in The Minories, Colchester, which contains a classic formulation of the principle, though the vocabulary by which he expresses it is in part outmoded.

He starts with the apparent truth that the skies in his paintings could not be, as he had been often advised, a white sheet behind the object. There is in the Victoria and Albert Museum a drawing of Sherborne Abbey which might almost have been made as a demonstration of this fact, for in it he has, most unusually, given no indication of a sky, and the result is surprisingly unbalanced and incomplete in effect. From this *reductio ad absurdum* he goes on to postulate that the sky creates the mood of the landscape below it. He had become quite aware that it was one of his main technical difficulties to make his skies sufficiently emphatic and relevant without their being too obtrusive, and it was for this reason, he says, that he had embarked on his large series of studies.

Quite apart from its consonance with the lighting of the earth, the sky has a purely ornamental effect in landscape painting. This is especially so in a country without mountains, the country of East Anglia or North London. The high climbing cumulus clouds, the wisp of cirrus or flocks of cirro-cumulus, the rich variations of colour through blue and silver-grey to white, and the satisfying, sculptural variations of form, provide as much pleasure for the eye as the contours of the ground, the play of light and shade on terrestrial objects or the ramification of the trees. The Dutch landscape painters of the seventeenth century, Jacob van Ruisdael chief among them, had understood the need for a marked feature in the upper levels of their pictures and Constable, painting similar cloud-dominated flats, had learned this lesson from them.

Skies also provide an element of free creation, or of variations within extremely wide limits, against the unchanging forms of the earth. Their constant mobility and change, to which northerners are sensitive from childhood, can be exploited by the artist who has an almost limitless number of painting effects to choose among. The desire to increase his range in the choice of potential skies was another of the motives leading to Constable's studies in the summer and autumn of 1821 and 1822. Although he would have repudiated the notion, there is an element of abstract expressionism about his pure sky subjects which links them to the twentieth century.

Constable was always interested in the floating scientific ideas of his time, in anatomy, geology, and the sciences of structure, and an additional impetus to his studies was probably given by the publication in 1820 of Luke Howard's CLIMATE OF LONDON, in which wider currency was first given to the author's now familiar classification of cloud forms into cumulus, stratus and so on. Certainly Constable knew of this new nomenclature, since he wrote the word 'cirrus' on the back of one of his cloud studies. Such an interest would accord with his pronouncement that all pictures should be scientific experiments. But the skies which he was studying in the interest of greater truth to Nature through the intense observation of facts became in the end romantic symbols in their own right. A stormy sky was not merely the cause of murky shadows and dully lit foliage; it was an apparent metaphor for the human mind in distress. At first Constable was uniformly optimistic in his use of the sky as a symbol; the sameness of effect for which Fisher had reproached him was that of a serene, sunny, summer morning. But even by 1823 he had put so rainy a sky behind his *Salisbury Cathedral from the Bishop's Grounds* that Dr Fisher, with the tastes of an earlier generation, could not live with it. Ultimately Constable had to paint two variants; a small-scale one, brimming over with sunshine, as a wedding present for the Bishop's daughter, and a full-size one with a less stormy sky for the Bishop himself.

The addiction to dramatic, tempestuous skies grew on Constable as he got older, and it is not hard to correlate the climax of this process with the illness and death of his wife and the increasing troubles of his later life. Nothing confirms this more strikingly than a comparison of the mezzotints made by David Lucas from 1830 onwards with the earlier originals; in many cases, such as those of the large canal scenes, the summer of the early 1820s has been emphatically replaced by storm.

The image in which his sense of the romantic expressiveness of the sky took its final form was the rainbow. He had started to study this as early as 1812 when he was in Suffolk; and he took up the theme again with passion in his fifties with a sense that it summed up his feeling for light, colour, and the natural beauty following on a storm. Because he always looked for analogues to his tastes among the old masters he enthusiastically embraced Rubens's use of the same symbol in such pictures as the 'Rainbow Landscape', now in the Wallace Collection. As he said in one of his lectures, 'By the Rainbow of Rubens, I do not allude to a particular picture, for Rubens often introduced it; I mean, indeed, more than the rainbow itself, I mean dewy light and freshness, the departing shower, with the exhilaration of the returning sun.'

When he painted his Hampstead sky and cloud studies Constable reverted to the practice he had first adopted in the Lake District of writing on the back of the sketches a description of the weather and of its development. Though hardly as systematic as his contemporary John Dalton's daily records of rainfall maintained for fifty-seven years, these provide a dipping check into the relation between skies and weather sufficient for the artist's own use. They range from such comments of high actuality as 'Noon. Very sultry, with large drops of rain falling on my palette; light air from S.W.', to – 'Noon. Wind fresh at West. Sun very hot. Looking southward exceedingly bright, vivid and glowing; very heavy showers in the afternoon but a fine evening. High wind in the night'. The second of these shows the extent to which Constable followed up the pattern of the day's weather, and the obvious deduction that it was written on the back of the sketch some time after it was painted is confirmed by the fact that it replaces an erased inscription describing a different day. The inscription on the back of another cloud study, now in the National Gallery of Victoria, 'Very appropriate to the coast at Osmington', shows how he kept looking at them as a repertory of possible skies for other compositions; he must have made this sketch five or six years after his only visit to the Dorset coast.

Now that the large paintings of the River Stour have been analysed, the place of the oil sketches Constable painted in the open air can be more fully understood. They are certainly complete artistic statements, and communicate an aesthetic pleasure in which no element is lacking. But the high value which the painter himself placed upon them derived from their being the essential first steps to the making of larger, fully considered compositions; they were to him the raw materials of his art. They are an exact counterpart to his pencil drawings, if we make the necessary allowance for the fact that in them he was concerned not merely with tone but with the full colour range of the scene before him. Even the merits of the oil sketches arise from conditions similar to those of the drawings. When working in the open air, in front of the motif, Constable was in a state of heightened consciousness, rapt in a species of hypnotic vision. The depth of that concentration is engagingly exemplified by the story of how he was once sitting so still that a field mouse crept into his pocket unobserved. This trance-like state gave rapidity to his grasp of the scene before him, and unity to his visual apperception of it.

It is unlikely that Constable was aware of his predecessors in the genre of the open-air landscape sketch: Desportes and Valenciennes in the eighteenth-century French school, for instance. The impulse towards his sketches seems to have grown logically out of his own reflections and ambitions. In fact, the process can be seen at work in the first natural paintings he made in Dedham Vale in 1802, and in a rather different way in the work he carried out in the Lake District in 1806. While the greater part of this was in water-colour, it was in the few oil sketches he made on that journey that we have been able to discern the beginnings of his mature style.

The early 1820s witnessed the full fruition of the friendship between John Constable and John Fisher; the imaginative acts of patronage by which the latter bought *The White Horse* and *Stratford Mill* were not undertaken as a *placebo* but as a genuine act of judgement. The mutual confidence between these two like-minded people gives their correspondence its freedom and self-revelatory power. For Constable it was a sort of confessional, his chief avenue of expression for the ambitions, frustrations, affections, and aversions which he could not talk about to his family or his other friends. The letters they exchanged have survived in large part and form an essential key to the understanding of his character and thought. The absolute freedom with which Constable wrote developed to the full the acid wit and biting phrase which was the natural expression of his brooding, somewhat cynical mind; and John Fisher was, though idle, a cultivated man of much originality of mind. The correspondence has its moments of absurdity when it verges upon the ultra-conservatism of either writer:

Fisher was a blue-print of the early nineteenth-century
Establishment and Constable a Tory of the deepest dye,
thrown into paroxysms of fear by the agitation for Reform.
In this mood Constable would deliver himself of such
splendours of pomposity as 'that one short sentence marks
you master of your own profession' when discussing Fisher's
views on the Dissenters.

More frequently the letters have a genuine humour, for
instance when Constable begins 'The dignitary of the
Church has forgotten the dignitary of the easel', or when
Fisher says 'Think of St Paul with a full blown wig, deep
shovel hat, apron, round belly, double chin, deep cough,
stern eye, rough voice and imperious manner, drinking port
wine and laying down the law, of the best way for escap-
ing the operation of the Curates' Residence Act', and again,
'Pity me. I am sitting in the shade ... with a quiet stomach
and cool head: and I am obliged to leave all this to go ten
miles to eat venison and drink claret with a brother officer
whose head is filled with the same sort of materials that his
venison pasty is made of.' Some of Fisher's wit still strikes
the mark: 'Men do not purchase pictures because they
admire them, but because others covet them'; 'Do not
despise (the newspapers) too much. They cannot give you
fame, but they attend on her. Smoke gives notice that the
house is afire.'

The perfect confidence between the two friends made it
possible for Fisher to give help to Constable in almost all
the crises of his life, until his own untimely death in 1832.
His insistence on Constable's marriage, and his purchase of
the first two large landscapes have been mentioned. His
help was to be felt again when the death of Mrs Constable
was so shattering a blow to his friend. It is thanks to this
lack of reserve that we know so much more of the inner
workings of Constable's mind, and the day-to-day alloca-
tion of his time, than of almost any previous painter;
Delacroix, who is generally thought of as the first to be
fully self-revealed in his writings, being of a younger
generation.

From time to time after his marriage Constable stayed

with Fisher; latterly Mrs Constable showed signs of jealousy at the amount of time he spent in Salisbury. The most productive of these visits was the one he paid for the greater part of July and August 1820, when in addition to making some oil sketches of the Cathedral he used at least three sketch-books to record views of Salisbury and the places he visited from that centre. Thus there are some sensitive drawings of Gillingham, and a study of Stonehenge from which sixteen years later he made one of his last exhibits at the Royal Academy. The following year he accompanied Fisher on his Archidiaconal visitation of Berkshire, this time using a larger sketch-book, the pages of which measured $6\frac{3}{4} \times 10\frac{1}{4}$ in. The drawings he made in the Berkshire sketch-book differ in intention and therefore also in style from those of the previous year. Shortly after filling the small pocket sketch-book of 1814 Constable had adopted the practice of making more completely realized studies in pencil on a somewhat larger paper: these drawings, which are of great softness and subtlety, cover such subjects as Osmington in 1816, East Bergholt, Mistley and Colchester in 1817, Hampstead and Salisbury in 1820. While on the journey of 1821 he did not abate any of his search for detail or delicacy of outline, he added water-colour or grey washes to a number of them, and the extent to which he carried the pencil drawing shows that they were conceived with this addition in mind. Although he had washed a few of his Osmington drawings he had not systematically made tinted drawings since his visits to the Peak District in 1801 and the Lakes in 1806. The subjects so treated range over the whole extent of Fisher's four deaneries – Newbury, Reading, Wallingford, and Abingdon – and include studies of Blenheim and Oxford. As we would expect, he devoted most attention to the canal at Newbury which, with its locks, mills, barges and tree-shadowed towpaths provided the nearest analogy to the banks of the Stour. None of these drawings was made up into an oil composition, and it may be that Constable washed them the more carefully so that they might exist in their own right.

In the same year, after his first extensive bout of 'skying' at Hampstead, Constable made a late autumn visit to see Fisher at Salisbury, arriving on 8 November. He was by now committed to painting *Salisbury Cathedral from the Bishop's Grounds* for Bishop Fisher, and was refreshing his memory of the scene before facing the completion of this task. At the same time he visited Winchester and made two washed sketches of the Cathedral there. An unusual product of this visit is the sketch, completed on to a second page (both in the Victoria and Albert Museum), of the priest-vicar of Salisbury Cathedral, the Rev. Edmund Benson, wearing a chasuble. Figure drawings, even portrait drawings of this kind, occur not infrequently in Constable's work, but the odd thing about this drawing is that the priest, who might even in so unliturgical an age have been expected to know better, is wearing the fifteenth-century vestment back to front.

The pertinacity of Constable's study of familiar scenes is brought out by another drawing he made during this November visit to Salisbury, showing the bridge at the suburb of Harnham and the old houses at its right-hand end. He made a drawing of the same scene from an almost identical viewpoint eight years later, on his last visit to Fisher; then, in 1831, the day after he had been present at the Coronation of William IV, he took out the two drawings and strengthened the water-colour washes of the original version, duly noting the course of events on its back.

The demands of his work, his growing family and Mrs Constable's failing health then had their effect in reducing the practicability of these refreshing visits. Between 1821 and 1829 (the year after his wife's death), Constable could make only one stay at Salisbury. It was in 1823, and this time Maria, the most uncomplaining of wives, grudged the days he spent away from her. Constable excused to Fisher his arrival a day before time by comparing it with the practice of the surgeon Astley Cooper, who would come an hour sooner than the time fixed for an operation to save the patient some of the horrors of anticipation. On this occasion he went with Fisher to Beckford's neo-Gothic palace, Fonthill, to Gillingham again, and to Sherborne.

He was looking for a subject at Gillingham; J. P. Tinney, the lawyer to whom Fisher had given *Stratford Mill*, had asked Constable to paint him two upright landscapes. The commission was beginning to fidget Constable, who disliked being bound in this way, and who was having difficulty in borrowing back his large painting as frequently as he wished. But it was still in being, and he lighted upon Perne's Mill at Gillingham with which Tinney had a family connection, as the theme for one of these pictures. The following year, after a final row with Tinney in which Fisher tried to see fair play, Constable was released from his engagement; but none the less he painted a small horizontal view of the mill for Fisher (now in the Fitzwilliam Museum), repeated it on a somewhat larger scale for the Royal Academy Exhibition of 1828 (now in the Paul Mellon Collection) and made a different view into a vertical composition, apparently first shown at the British Institution in 1827 and now in the Victoria and Albert Museum.

The year 1823 was altogether eventful for the artist. It began with his serious illness, and with his completing the Bishop's picture; now, after the visit to Fisher in August he was invited by Sir George Beaumont to stay at his Leicestershire seat, Coleorton. This visit gave Constable one of the most intense periods of pleasure he had ever experienced. The only discordant note was the rather fretful tone of his wife's letters; she understood why he kept on delaying his return, but reproached him for having stayed unnecessarily long with Fisher in the summer. In spite of the overpowering tug homewards, Constable, though the most uxorious of men, stayed on; he left home on 24 October, intending to remain only a short time; in fact, his visit lasted five weeks, till 28 November.

Strong character though Constable was, he always remained to some extent in subjection to Beaumont, whose early appreciation and admirable collection had fired his enthusiasm for painting; and Leslie tells us, with some indignation, that throughout his life Beaumont always adopted towards Constable the posture of a teacher. But courteous and deferential though he was, Constable had as much independence in the defence of his own art as the democratically inclined Leslie. It was apparently on this visit that he made the most famous riposte in art criticism when, in response to Beaumont's recommendation of the colour of an old Cremona fiddle for the prevailing tone of a landscape, he laid an old violin on the green lawn before the house.

The pleasure Constable took in the visit was not derived from the fact that he was staying in the country house of a rich man who enjoyed a higher rank in the social scale. It was due primarily to the delight he found in Sir George's consummate collection of seventeenth-century landscape painting and, hardly less strongly, to the genuine respect he had for his host and hostess, and in particular for the methodical assiduity with which Beaumont applied himself to painting. It was generally known that, had he not been a landowner, he would have been an outstanding professional artist. And though their ideas in matters of taste did not agree, Constable much admired the regularity of this daily routine and the systematic way in which his host applied himself both to painting and to connoisseurship. The lesson, could he have benefited from it, was precisely what he needed, for he himself was the most unsystematic of men. Both Fisher and Beaumont urged him to get fresh air and exercise, to take regular meals and purge himself of worry, and to throw the loungers and gossips out of his painting-room, but he was incapable of following this well-meant advice. A congenital obsessive, when preoccupied with a problem in his painting he would gnaw away at it all day. When he did go out on business in London his attention was so much distracted by objects which caught his fancy that he sauntered rather than walked. To this mode of life Sir George Beaumont's household, run like clock-work, seemed the antithesis; and yet its master was able to produce a great many paintings by adhering to his rigid programme. In a mood of self-criticism engendered by seeing him at work Constable vowed never again to be angry, impatient or peevish, and considered that the visit had made him 'so much more of an artist'.

More fundamental than these good resolutions for reform, which were soon forgotten, was the pleasure he got from the paintings by Claude, Poussin, Wilson, and J. R. Cozens in Beaumont's collection. Here again there is an inconsistency in his attitude. Beaumont gave many of these paintings to the National Gallery, an institution which Constable deplored because he thought it would breed a race of picture-copyists and mannered imitators of the Old Masters. Yet he himself had the most exquisite perception of the beauties of these landscapes, and set to work to copy two of the Claudes, as well as to pore over as many as he could of the prints and drawings in the house. The drawings included some by Beaumont, and he copied a few of those which had been made at Dedham. He wrote to his wife: 'You would laugh to see my bedroom; I have dragged so many things into it, books, portfolios, prints, canvases, pictures.' And it was his anxiety to finish his Claude copies which caused him to overrun the original length of his stay.

With so much study and copying he did not spend as much time as he would have wished in the open air. None the less he rode over to Staunton Harold, a ruined house of Lord Ferrer's, and made a fine drawing near by. As he recorded on the back of the sketch, Sir George Beaumont held his horse while he made it. He made a drawing of Coleorton Hall in Miss Southey's album, and other drawings in the park. Beaumont had conceived a fondness of dedicating memorials in his grounds to famous painters, and these were a natural magnet for Constable, both because they were embowered in trees and because he too venerated his famous forerunners. Even so he did not record them till the last day of his visit. His study of the stone dedicated to Sir George's master, Richard Wilson, went no farther than the drawing in the Victoria and Albert Museum, but that of the Cenotaph to Sir Joshua Reynolds, a more considerable erection, he used as the basis of the large oil he exhibited at the Royal Academy in 1836. Wordsworth had composed verses for the monument, which were inscribed upon the altar, and these lines were transcribed by the artist on the back of his drawing.

Constable's respect for the Academy was intensified by the difficulty he experienced in gaining acceptance by that body, and extended with particular fervour to its past. He showed his veneration for Sir Joshua Reynolds, its first President, in a practical way. A palette given by Reynolds to Beaumont was subsequently passed on to Lawrence, and included in the sale after his death. Constable bought it, and gave it to the Academy with an inscribed silver plate recording its history. The same devotion to the memory of the chief founder of the English school of painting led to his choice of *The Cenotaph* for the subject of one of his last paintings.

6

SUCCESS IN FRANCE

In 1824 Constable was 48 years old. It is interesting, as a comparison of the different courses which genius takes, to recall that this was the age at which Shakespeare had left London for Stratford to spend the last four years of his life in retirement. After the slow development of his powers Constable was now in the most productive section of his career, and his fame was beginning to spread. He first tasted its full sweetness this year through the exhibition of three of his paintings, *The Hay Wain*, the *View on the Stour near Dedham*, and an unidentified view of Hampstead, at the Paris Salon.

The train of events which led to this honour had begun in 1821 when the French critic, Charles Nodier, wrote an enthusiastic account, for publication in Paris, of *The Hay Wain*, which he had seen at the Summer Exhibition of the Royal Academy. In the same year Géricault, so ardent an Anglophile, had come to England to exhibit his 'Raft of the Medusa'. Whereas Constable could only see in the modern French school works formed from 'the scaffold, the hospital and a bawdy house', Géricault, when he returned to France, told Delacroix that he was entirely astounded by *The Hay Wain*. It seems that the decision to exhibit this picture in Paris was planned to some extent as a tribute to Géricault, who had died early in 1824. Other causes had also been at work. John Arrowsmith, who, despite his English-sounding name, was a Parisian art dealer, had begun to import smaller works by Constable into France, and had been trying for some time to buy *The Hay Wain* for less than its full price. The relationship between artist and dealer began with a wrangle when Arrowsmith offered a low price for the painting when he saw it at the British Institute in 1822: 'It is too bad to allow myself to be knocked down by a Frenchman,' said Constable. But it blossomed into a favourable one for the artist; he probably received more commissions from Arrowsmith than from any other single source, and the dealer's 'Constable room' was for a number of years an attraction for French artists. The connection led to the introduction of another French dealer, Claude Schroth, who also bought a number of Constable's paintings for sale to the collectors of his country. Although adverse economic conditions caused both dealers to cease these imports late in 1826, there was for a time a steady flow of his pictures to France, some of them repetitions of prototypes he had already made popular. Sea-pieces, and views of Hampstead Heath, seem to have been especially sought after.

The episode shows that, although it was in an embryonic form in comparison with the efficient machine it later became, the world of the French dealer was beginning to make its presence felt, and was showing that acuteness and adventurousness which led to the long predominance of Paris as a centre of contemporary art. No English dealer in Constable's time bothered to do more than look at his exhibits in the annual exhibition and occasionally to commission a replica. In four or five years Arrowsmith and Schroth bought over twenty paintings from him, sold them successfully, and enlivened French art by their adventurous policy. The flow of commissions kept Constable at full stretch and contributed to his feeling that at last he had attained success and recognition.

The highlights in all this activity was, of course, the actual display of *The Hay Wain* and the *View on the Stour* at the Salon, with the consequence that they led to great critical discussion, mainly favourable, and that the pictures, after being moved to a better position, were awarded a gold medal by Charles X. Most important of all is the effect upon Delacroix, leading to his repainting of the 'Scènes de Massacre de Scio' which hung in the same exhibition.

Although few things are more difficult to establish than the influence exercised by one artist upon a contemporary, the fruitful encounter of Constable and Delacroix is thoroughly well documented. It had begun earlier than

1824, when Delacroix had heard of Géricault's enthusiasm and then in 1823 saw a sketch by Constable in the collection of Régnier – the first work by the English artist we know of in Paris. The interest these events aroused culminated in the arrival of *The Hay Wain* and its companions. These were visible at Arrowsmith's gallery before the Salon opened in August. As soon as he had seen them Delacroix realized that he wished to bring more light into his painting, and that he could do so by adopting some of the principles of Constable's technique.

In *The Hay Wain* the green meadow in the middle distance is painted in a gamut of colours ranging from yellow through green to blue; the red roof of the cottage has elements of white, yellow, and dark brown; the water is composed of dark-grey, yellowish-brown and thin white streaks, while the muddy path, predominantly brown in the foreground, ranges from red to grey. This use of broken tints, often applied in small, crisp, dry touches, and sometimes with a vertical striation or fracture which gives further life to the surface texture of the paint, suggested to Delacroix the way to lighten his own rather sombre composition. Hence he hatched significant sections of 'The Massacre of Chios' – the arm of the old woman, her skirt, the dead infant – with small touches of pure resonant colour, and achieved the result at which he was aiming by bringing greater luminosity to his canvas.

The effect upon Delacroix of the paintings by Constable which were in Paris in 1824 was not the final stage in their relationship. In the next year Delacroix came to England – he was a passionate Anglophile and dandy – and was resolved to meet the artists he most admired, Wilkie, Lawrence, Copley Fielding, and Constable. To assist his meeting with Constable, Schroth had provided him with a letter in which he told Constable of the great effect his picture had had in Paris and explained that the bearer was a young artist who greatly admired his work and wished to meet him. Unfortunately Constable was away when he first attempted to present this letter; but it is almost certain that the Englishman and Frenchman met eventually. For one thing, the letter of introduction is actually in the Constable family's correspondence – and Delacroix was well known for the persistence with which he pursued his ends. For another, there is in the Louvre a sketch-book apparently used by Constable at Brighton around 1825, which subsequently belonged to Delacroix. Finally, nine years after Constable's death, Delacroix recorded the crux of what he had learned from Constable in this way: 'Constable says that the superiority of the green of his meadows comes from its being composed of a multitude of different greens. The lack of intensity and life in the foliage of most landscape paintings arises because they usually paint them with a uniform tone.' Now, we know that Constable had derived this doctrine from J. T. Smith's views on the picturesque, though he developed the idea and fully made it his own in his practice. But it is unlikely that Delacroix can have gleaned it from a written source, and it is reasonable to assume from the form in which he records the statement that he had himself heard it from Constable's own lips. In that case he probably saw in the painter's studio not only the full-scale sketch for *The Hay Wain* but also the sketch for *The Leaping Horse*, which carried the liberation of technique farther than anything yet seen in England or conceived in France. Delacroix never lost his youthful enthusiasm and as late as 1858 wrote to Théophile Silvestre: 'Constable, homme admirable, est une des gloires anglaises.'

The question of the permanent effect of the vogue for Constable on French landscape painting usually creates more heat than light. It is a problem frequently conceived in the wrong terms, as it is when it is taken for granted that, should there be any such influence, it must be one exercised directly upon the Impressionists. Attempts to establish this have generally foundered upon Pissarro's old-age memories of his exile in England in 1870, when according to his account he and Monet admired Turner, whose aims they thought similar to their own, but saw no particular novelty in Constable.

The facts are rather different. It is demonstrably true that the sight of Constable's pictures was a revelation to the young French landscape painters of the 1820s. Paul Huet's 'Château et Ville d'Eu' in the collection of M. Pierre Miquel is an almost direct transcription of Constable's *Hampstead Heath: Branch Hill Pond*, varied to the smallest amount necessary to fit it to the topography of a different scene. Théodore Rousseau was, in his sketches, another follower; Troyon was so great an admirer that he tried to buy the sketches for *The Hay Wain* and *The Leaping Horse* now in the Victoria and Albert Museum. Before Constable's pictures were shown at the Salon in 1824 the official French style of landscape was typified by the enamel-like finish and the classical formulae of C. Vernet and J. Swebach-Desfontaines. Constable himself described their method as a sort of *découpage*; they made separate studies of the individual components of a landscape and stuck them together without considering the general effect. He was not the only English exemplar to counteract this style: Bonington, Lawrence, Copley Fielding all played their part. But the different degrees of immediacy, vitality, wholeness of effect, and naturalism of colour which we see in Huet, Troyon, Rousseau, Millet, Chintreuil, and Boudin is due in very large measure to him. Since the Impressionists built on the foundation of these forerunners, they are only affected by Constable unconsciously and at second remove. The degree of similarity between their freshness and natural colour and Constable's is partly due to this ancestry, partly due to their pursuing the same intentions, partly an historical accident. For, in fact, the immediately visible similarities which appear to make Constable a direct anticipator of the Impressionists' discoveries are only superficial. The Impressionists painted on a light ground on a high gamut of colour and aimed at transcribing an immediate, passing, effect. The division of tones they practised, and which Pissarro quite correctly did not find in Constable, was based on the theory of optical mixture; two touches of different colour side by side blending into a third colour in the spectator's eye. Constable painted over a dark, generally reddish-brown, ground with bold strokes, each of which expressed an unambiguous colour. In his exhibited pictures he aimed at the typical and universal rather than the passing effect; and the division of tones which had so fired Delacroix gave a rich, broken, many-coloured texture but not the optical mixture of pure Impressionism.

Constable's reactions to his success in Paris were characteristic of his insular obstinacy and show the John Bull side of his nature in the ascendant. 'Think of the lovely valleys mid the peaceful farmhouses of Suffolk forming a scene of exhibition to amuse the gay and frivolous Parisians,' was his comment. The combined persuasion of his dealers and John Fisher could not induce him to go to France either to receive the congratulations of the artists who admired his works or later to accept the gold medal from the hands of Charles X. 'They cannot get at me on this side of the water and I shall not go there,' was his final word. Accordingly he was not present at the scene recorded in the painting by F.-J. Heim in the Louvre, showing King Charles X making presentations to other artists honoured at the same time. None the less he was anxious enough to receive his medal to write for it, when it was delayed, and it remained with him and his family as an object of great pride. Two years later, in 1826, he lent *The White Horse* (without bothering to tell Fisher that it had gone direct from his studio) to an exhibition at Lille and was again awarded a gold medal. The citation spoke of the 'raciness and originality of the style, which being founded in nature is capable of much beauty but dangerous to all imitators'.

Brighton, to which Constable had first in 1824 taken his wife and family of five children, was chosen by him for its better air. His eldest boy, John, had been seriously ill, and his wife was always delicate; as her consumption developed it was his wish to move her to the South Coast if she was fit enough to travel. As a resort he hated it. He found it Piccadilly by the seaside, 'the receptacle of the fashion and off-scouring of London', the surrounding countryside struck him as 'hideous masses of unfledged earth', and all he found for a painter was 'the breakers and sky'. Even these he thought unsuitable as serious subjects of picture-making;

seascapes seemed to him to be ousting landscapes at the Academy because of their obviousness.

In spite of these strictures the group of oil sketches which he made on the beach at Brighton in 1824 and subsequent years occupy an especially important place in his work, being both original and quite personal. To find the nearest analogy to them elsewhere we have to look not at the contemporary English practitioners of the seascape, such as Copley Fielding, Bonington, and Clarkson Stanfield, but at the rare sea-pieces of Delacroix and the oil sketches made by Boudin from the 1850s. To them Constable brought all the assurance in sky painting he had acquired by his massive studies in Hampstead in 1821 and 1822, with the result that they are fresh and unlaboured. By choosing a pinkish-grey ground lighter than his usual priming, over which he painted thinly, he preserved the luminosity of the scene, which was in a higher key over the southern sea than over the inland fields of Essex or Hampstead. With equal assurance he made an exceptionally large number of washed drawings with pen outline of the beaches, the skies and the colonies of fishing-boats on the shore or out at sea.

Arrowsmith was keenly aware of the interest French collectors took in seascapes, and having seen one of the sketch-books Constable kept in his first year at Brighton proposed that a series of drawings made up from them should be engraved by S. W. Reynolds and published in Paris. Though the project came to nothing, it sowed the seed which led to the engravings by David Lucas for ENGLISH LANDSCAPE SCENERY five years later.

Though Brighton never entered deeply into his affections, Constable did make one six-foot canvas from its scenery in which he profited from the experience gained from his considerable amount of preliminary oil sketching and drawing on the southern coast. This work is *The Marine Parade and Chain Pier, Brighton*, which he exhibited at the Royal Academy in 1827 and which is now in the Tate Gallery. No full-scale sketch is known for this painting, though there are oil studies for the composition, and also a pencil study which shows the working out of the composition. This

bears some evidence that Constable had difficulty in deciding how to finish his picture on the left, and an engraving
of the exhibited picture shows that it was at one time more
extensive on this side, and that someone – perhaps the
artist – has reduced it by removing a large sail and a standing figure which originally closed in the design at this
edge. The section of beach chosen for the scene was slight-
ingly described by the artist: 'The genteeler part, the Marine
Parade is still more unnatural, with its trimmed and neat
appearance, and the dandy jetty or Chain Pier with its long
and elegant strides into the sea a full quarter of a mile.' The
pier, in fact, fascinated Constable, taking the place in this
picture of the mills or barns he would use in his country
scenes, while in the foreground a clutter of anchors, up-
turned boats, baskets, and spars corresponds to the river-
rotted stakes and dams which he had formerly painted. For
the rest, the subject of the picture is, in his own phrase, 'the
breakers and sky', and the scene is animated by the blustery
wind and the rapid stormy clouds. In spite of the comparative unfamiliarity of the subject to him, he made of it one of
his most successful large paintings; but the increasing impression of unrest about the scene shows how his mind was
turning to troubled and melancholy preoccupations. This
aspect was over-emphasized even in the eyes of some who
admired and supported his work. John Fisher, who had
defended the storm clouds of Salisbury Cathedral against
the Bishop's complaints said of this picture when writing to
the artist after Maria Constable's death: 'Mellow its feroci-
ous beauties. Calm your mind and your sea at the same time
and let in sunshine and serenity.'

In the year in which this fine breezy seascape was
painted he had at last found a permanent home in Hampstead. He pitched upon a four-storey house in Well Walk;
from his painting-room at the top he was able to look direct
into the Thames Valley and to see the dome of St Paul's
riding its frequent mists. Although he had never been out
of England, Constable felt able to declare that the drawing-
room commanded the best view in Europe, adding in his
enthusiasm: 'The dome of St Paul's in the air realizes

Michelangelo's idea on seeing that of the Pantheon "I will build such a thing in the sky".' This house which replaced the lodgings he had taken in Hampstead year by year, enabled him to let most of his Charlotte Street house, though he kept the painting-room, the gallery, and some other rooms.

Through all his preoccupation with small seascapes and Hampstead scenes for Paris, and with making a great composition from the coastal scene at Brighton, Constable did not forget the Suffolk countryside, though for a time he had had his fill of canal scenes. To find the main successor to *The Lock* we have to go back to the year before the production of *The Marine Parade and Chain Pier, Brighton.* In 1826 he exhibited at the Royal Acadamy the painting now known as *The Cornfield.* It is an upright canvas, close in size to *The Lock* of 1824, and since Lucas engraved the two paintings as a pair, Constable may originally have intended it as a pendant to the earlier scene. However, in this he has moved away from the banks of the River Stour, and has chosen as his subject a lane leading from East Bergholt Church down the slopes of the valley towards Dedham, a path the artist had regularly taken as a schoolboy.

Once again the name by which the picture is known now is not that bestowed on it by its author; Constable was always careless about the titles of his pictures and preferred to refer to them by nicknames. In this case he dubbed the painting 'The Drinking Boy' in allusion to the figure slaking his thirst in the left foreground; he seems also to have called it 'my new lane'. When he first exhibited it he gave it the unhelpful title 'Landscape'. This he expanded at a second showing at the British Institution in 1827 as 'Landscape: Noon', adding a quotation from Thomson's 'Seasons':

A fresher gale
Begins to wave the wood, and stir the stream,
Sweeping with shadowy gust the fields of corn.

He had already given a garbled version of this quotation,

from memory, in a letter he wrote to Fisher on 8 April 1826, when he sent the painting to the Academy. This letter contains the fullest and most expressive references to the theme of the picture:

'inland, cornfields, a close lane kind of thing. But it is not neglected in any part; the trees are more than usually studied and the extremities well defined, as well as their species. They are shaken by a pleasant and healthful breeze *at Noon*'.

Constable has underlined the last two words in playful allusion to his dispute with Fisher about showing the same time of day in all his pictures; he has gone on driving his same nail, and not altered his plans to suit the public.

Just as the banks of the canal held the remembered joy of his childhood, this lane, along which he had walked daily to school, had a great reserve of emotion about it. The boy drinking from the stream, expressive of summer heat, may be a memory of his own idleness; certainly there is in the Tate Gallery a painting which contains this motif, but has no other connection with *The Cornfield*. As has been noted earlier, donkeys were always a source of pleasure to Constable, and he has introduced a mother and her foal into this painting; a rough oil sketch of this passage is in the Victoria and Albert Museum. In fact, these donkeys help to introduce the narrative interest of the picture, which, unlike his canal scene, is focused upon the animals. The attention of the young ass has been attracted by the boy drinking: the dog driving the sheep along the lane is looking at the foal and getting ready to bark at it. The sheep recall – though so obvious a motif need not be a reminiscence – the painting by Gaspar Poussin, 'Landscape near Albano' now in the National Gallery, a picture which made a profound impact when imported into England in 1800 and was copied by David Cox. Constable's *Green Lane* is a rendering in reverse of the same theme. He is not known to have made a full-scale sketch of the composition, which seems to have been enlarged from a small sketch from Nature, less than half-size. In converting this into its final form he introduced (rather surprisingly, so soon after his conversation with Beaumont) a dead tree in the left foreground, and placed a church in the distance. Dedham Church is not, in fact, in that position, but, just as in *The Leaping Horse*, he wanted a vertical feature there. The whole effect is as a mirror image of Claude's 'Hagar and the Angel' which he had admired so long, and was to remember again in 1828.

The choice of a quotation from Thomson is entirely consistent with the artist's admiration for this poet; he thought of him far more frequently than of Wordsworth, though the tenor of his work is more often compared with the latter's. But his admiration for 'The Seasons' did not degenerate into textual slavery, and the lines which he quotes refer to the fresher breezes of evening, not the hour of noon which the picture illustrates. The point which appealed to Constable was the linkage of wind with sun and ripening corn; he could never bear an airless landscape. At least he took the verses from the right season, 'Summer': his friend Phillips, a botanist at Brighton, consulted about the wild flowers which would be appropriate to the painting, wrote to him saying: 'I think it is July in your green lane. At this season all the tall grasses are in flower, bogrush, bullrush, teasel. The white bindweed now hangs its flowers over the branches of the hedge; the wild carrot and hemlock flower in banks of hedges, cow parsley, water plantain, etc. ...'

Constable concentrated as hard on the painting as on any he had produced; he described the process characteristically in his letter to Fisher: 'My picture occupied me wholly; I could think of and speak to no one. I felt like a relation of mine in the battle of Waterloo. He said he "dared not turn his head right or left, but always kept it straight forward, thinking of himself alone".' On another occasion he described it as having 'a little more eye-salve than I usually condescend to give'. In spite of its possession of this commodity it was not sold at the Academy exhibition and remained on his hands. Accordingly he included it among the paintings he sent to the Paris Salon in 1827.

This second excursion of Constable's into the Salon is
barely remembered, because it did not have the success
of novelty which attended his earlier appearance in 1824.
But some critics noticed his work, calmly, as a 'paysage
avec figures et animaux'.

More importantly, the comparatively ingratiating quality
of the picture led to its selection after his death as the first
painting to represent him in the National Gallery; and thus
as his first introduction to a more permanent and lasting
fame in England. The chairman of the fund which
presented *The Cornfield* to the nation was Constable's old
friend Sir William Beechey, the portrait painter. In 1831
Constable recounted to Lucas a visit Beechey had made
to him: 'Beechey was here yesterday, and said "Why damn
it Constable what a damned fine picture you are making;
but you look damned ill, and you have got a damned bad
cold".' But Beechey, who was twenty-three years older
than his friend, survived him, and his committee chose this
picture as a memorial. Some subscribers would have preferred the more adventurous choice of *Salisbury Cathedral
from the Meadows*, but it can hardly be doubted that *The
Cornfield* does the greater justice to him, and is peculiarly
appropriate as an embodiment of the pure rusticity of the
fields near his home.

In the autumn of 1827 he spent a holiday at Flatford
with his family, taking his two eldest children Maria
('Minna') and John with him. His brother Abram had been
apprehensive of their drowning in the mill-stream, but all
went well. Maria decided that Suffolk was much like Hampstead only the blackberries were finer, and Constable himself found he preferred his Well Walk house to any of his
family's. But the simple pleasure he took in this return to
his native county – his first long visit for nine years – is
evident enough in the large, balanced, reflective drawings
he made along the Stour.

The last comparatively carefree rendering he made of
that landscape was the *Dedham Vale* which he exhibited
at the Royal Academy in 1828. This is a large upright of
the same size as *The Cornfield*, and it is a final embodiment

of one of his favourite views, down the course of the Stour
to the sea from a point on Gun Hill. In writing of it to
Fisher Constable called it 'perhaps my best'. It is an open
panoramic view, and to make it he has adapted the main
lines of the early sketch, *Dedham Vale*, 1802, which was
one of his first achievements in a naturalistic vein. But he
had modified the composition to include a nearer bend of
the river and Stratford Bridge, with the old Talbooth Inn
on the Essex bank below it. A rather regrettable band of
gipsies in the foreground strikes a consciously picturesque
note.

7

THE RESTLESS CLOSE

THE year 1828 seemed to begin auspiciously for Constable. Although it was not sold, his chief painting at the Academy, *Dedham Vale*, was well received, and was even praised by the Press. His father-in-law, Charles Bicknell, died and, in spite of the hostility to Constable into which he had been weakly forced by Dr Rhudde at the time of his engagement to Maria, left him a fortune amounting to £20,000. This unexpected event left Constable and his family independent of the uncertain proceeds of his painting. His seventh and last child, Lionel Bicknell Constable, was born at the beginning of the year; another event of great joy to him, since he so loved children. But to be set against this were darker thoughts. He began on the hateful and humiliating task of soliciting votes for election as R.A., only to be told that he was not as good a painter as William Etty, who gained the vacancy. As he wrote to Leslie, 'I have heard so much of the higher walks of art that I am quite sick. I had my own opinions even on that – but I was desired to hold my tongue and not "argue the point".' The point at issue was the old one which enraged Constable quite legitimately – the view of the Academicians that landscape was a 'lower' form of painting than subject pictures.

But far more ominous was the deteriorating condition of Maria Constable's health. She had been consumptive for many years; now she began rapidly to decline. He brought her back from Brighton to London in August. Leslie visited them in Hampstead in November and gives an affecting account of how Constable was in his usual spirits in his wife's presence, but on his leaving took him into another room, wrung his hand and burst into tears without speaking.

Maria Constable died on 23 November 1828. She was only forty-one and had been married to John Constable for twelve years, in which time she had borne him four sons and three daughters. Although he had a reputation as the gallant 'handsome miller' when he was young, there is every indication that John Constable was entirely devoted and faithful to her. She had supplied the background of calm domesticity – 'my placid and contented companion' – which alone could counterpoise the energy of his temperament. Her death left an emotional void which was never filled. Leslie records that Constable wore mourning for the rest of his life; and the same abandonment to grief is seen in the greater lack of control in his paintings immediately following her death. But, although inwardly broken, Constable shouldered his responsibilities and continued with the development of his art. He had to face the necessity of bringing up his children, in whom he delighted, and laboured on under a stern sense of duty. Fisher wrote to console him as best he could: 'I write with the hope and intention of giving you comfort, but really I know not how', and after a few halting attempts turns the subject rather awkwardly to Schlegel's views on Gothic architecture.

In the midst of his troubles Constable had again to beg for the votes of the Academicians. This time, ironically enough, he was elected, although he wrote before canvassing for votes: 'I have little heart to face an ordeal (or rather should I not say run a gauntlet) in which kicks are kind treatment to those insults to the mind which we candidates, wretches of necessity, are exposed to, annually, from some high-minded members who stickle for the "elevated and noble" walks of art; i.e. preferring the shaggy posteriors of a Satyr to the moral feeling of landscape.' Lawrence, with less than his usual courtesy, showed that he considered Constable very lucky to be chosen before a number of prominent history painters, including Francis Danby; a snub which caused him to write: 'I am still smarting under my election.' Meanwhile a touch of unconscious comedy was supplied by the pious miniature painter Andrew Robertson, who wrote of his success in becoming an Academician: 'Having gained this election, you have nothing higher to look up to in this world', and urged his mind towards heavenly vistas.

It is hardly surprising that, although he managed to finish his new large painting *Hadleigh Castle* in time for the Academy, he was in doubt whether to send it in. In the event he did so, though with less critical success than in former years. To the catalogue entry he added an extract from Thomson's 'Summer', from a passage in the invocation to the sun's quickening power:

> 'The desert joys
> Wildly, through all his melancholy bounds,
> Rude ruins glitter; and the briny deep,
> Seen from some pointed promontory's top,
> Far to the blue horizon's utmost verge,
> Restless, reflects a floating gleam.'

The quotation is from the source which Constable had used for *The Cornfield* three years before; but the meaning he gives to it, and the tone of his painting, is very different from that smiling optimistic scene.

For the origin of the composition Constable went back to the sketch-book he had used fifteen years before when he had visited his old friend, the Rev. Mr Driffield, then vicar of Feering in Essex. While there, he had visited the coastal estuary of the Thames at Southend; it was the period of utmost difficulty in his courtship of Maria. In the sketch-book, whose pages measure $3\frac{1}{4} \times 4\frac{3}{8}$ in., he made a pencil drawing of Hadleigh Castle on its hill overlooking the estuary near Southend, and it was to this he turned when composing his large picture. The sea had sad associations for him; he had written of Southend to Maria: 'I was always delighted with the melancholy grandeur of a seashore', and it may have been the combination of these associations, his separation from Maria and the melancholy of the sea, which led him to his choice of subject. Thomson's verses are couched in a much higher pitch of romantic feeling than the actual scene of Constable's picture would suggest. The poet is evidently thinking of a vertiginously lofty castle; but Hadleigh is only 150 ft above the level of the plain. None the less, the scene is an evocative one, and

Constable has extracted the last vestige of expression by the stormy sky and the cold sinister light. To him the picture had no fixed title; sometimes it was the 'Nore', sometimes the 'Ruin', with the added implication that it might be his own ruin he had painted.

The version he exhibited disappeared from view for over seventy years, and has only just emerged in the collection of Mr and Mrs Paul Mellon. For this reason, the composition has long been judged in England by the full-scale sketch in the Tate Gallery, which exploits to the full the Expressionistic ruggedness and the cold, almost monochrome tonality which is the basis of the painter's conception. The final version, closely followed by Lucas's mezzotint, is as it were the sketch put firmly into focus, so that the two remaining towers of the castle, the hill on which it stands, the River Thames below, and the hills in the distance are all seen with far greater clarity. He has increased the sense of height by introducing, in both the sketch and the final version, birds wheeling below eye-level so that the spectator's vision is drawn down to them.

In the same year, 1829, Constable embarked upon the publication of a series of plates after his oil sketches and paintings, to which he gave the name ENGLISH LANDSCAPE SCENERY. This was a momentous decision, which had a great effect upon his immediate life and his posthumous repute; and it is hard to tell whether the evils it undoubtedly brought in its train are outweighed by the benefits. Some such project had been mooted before, in 1824, at the height of Constable's Parisian fame. As well as proposing to engrave twelve drawings of Brighton coast scenes, S. W. Reynolds wanted to make a mezzotint of *The Lock*. Fisher expressed his doubts about the proposal: 'There is in your pictures too much evanescent effect, and general tone, to be expressed by black and white. Your charm is colour and the cool tint of English daylight. The burr of mezzotint will never touch that.' The scheme fell through, and S. W. Reynolds died soon after; but the idea had been implanted in Constable's mind, and when he wished to pursue it further he sent for a young man who had been Reynolds's apprentice, David Lucas.

One of the motives which actuated him may have been a desire to emulate Turner's LIBER STUDIORUM. This venture had been started by Turner nearly a quarter of a century before, in 1806, at a time when the ambitious young artist had conceived that it would make a permanent centre for his posthumous fame. Two points about the publication are relevant to Constable's project. The first is that it aimed at being a systematic survey of the categories of landscape. Although Turner's mental powers, and those of his advisers, did not permit this to lead to any significant result, the intention may well have been at the back of Constable's plan. Secondly, Turner rejected aquatint as a medium and chose mezzotint, reinforced by an etched outline, for the translation into monochrome of his compositions. The engraver of one of the last published plates of the LIBER STUDIORUM was S. W. Reynolds; it was he who had planned to mezzotint Constable's *The Lock*, and his pupil David Lucas did, in fact, carry the entire burden of the production of ENGLISH LANDSCAPE SCENERY. Perhaps, when he was choosing the medium, he remembered that his wife had written to him about some prints, 'They are done in mezzotinto, which I am *particularly fond of*.'

To understand the effectiveness as representations of Constable of the plates in this publication, and to grasp at the same time their dangers for him and for posterity, it is necessary to consider the nature of the mezzotint medium in which they were reproduced. To make a mezzotint a copper plate is in the first instance pitted in many directions with a uniform system of close dots, so that if inked and printed it will produce on the paper an impression of rich, velvety black. By scraping down the pitted ridges round the dots any variant of tone can be produced from this black (the untouched plate) through all grades of grey to dead white (when the rim round the dots and the pit-hole itself has been eradicated). The method, invented in the seventeenth century, had been brought to perfection as a reproductive method by the eighteenth-century English engravers who copied the portraits of Reynolds, Gainsborough, and Romney, and is still known on the Continent as *la manière noire* or *la manière anglaise.*

To the extent that Constable was concentrating on chiaroscuro, or the balance between light and dark, in his paintings, the mezzotint was an ideal method of rendering his work. But it held special dangers, into which he fell all too completely. If you scratch at a mezzotint plate you introduce a light; Constable was becoming more and more obsessed by the broken accents on the particles of trees, grasses and foreground objects (as his increasing use of the palette knife shows) and could not resist the continual revision of his plates. He had always found it difficult to finish paintings on his easel; we have seen how frequently he worked on them after their return from the Royal Academy. With a mezzotint there was virtually no limit to the extent to which he could fidget about with his effects of light and dark. His constant retouchings and indecisions must have driven Lucas to distraction: it is small wonder that the engraver ended up as a pauper and a drunkard. It is the universal practice to make a number of trial prints or 'proofs' so that the engraver can examine the progress of his work; the sight of these frequently suggested changes in composition to Constable. The lists of proof states of these mezzotints therefore encompasses a great number and variety of alterations.

The tendency towards the distortion of his work by its reproduction in mezzotint was increased by his undertaking the task at this time. He was still reeling from the shock of his wife's death, and his inability to concentrate showed itself in his chronic indecision over the subjects to be included in the scenes of plates. His disturbed state of mind showed itself again in the instinct to make the skies darker, more stormy, with increased cloud and thin vertical lines of falling rain. Finally, there is a difficulty connected with Fisher's objection: 'Your charm is colour.' In a mezzotint a large dark-grey area may mean, on the earth, a grassy bank, the shadowy green banks of a river, or the shade on a gravelled path. In the sky the same colour may stand for an intense blue, or for exactly its own shade of grey or black – that is, a storm cloud. Granted the mood in which Constable produced the plates, emphasizing the stormier aspects of nature, and the tendency of the mind to interpret as much as it can literally, the result is that most of the subjects, even if they started off as studies of a serene, noontide, summer's day, seem to have been steeped in Stygian gloom, and currency is given to a much more depressive and melancholic view of Constable's temperament and art than is warranted by his more mature and typical works.

It can hardly be laid as a fault at Constable's door that the mezzotints in ENGLISH LANDSCAPE SCENERY have been the major source for fakers of his work. Yet it is scarcely an exaggeration to say that his painting is more frequently assessed (and admired) from imitations of these plates than from his originals. These imitations, and they are extremely numerous, have a flashy facility which has charmed many a collector, yet their origin is generally apparent to anyone who has studied the question deeply.

A comparison of one or two of the mezzotints with their originals will help to show within what limits they reproduce Constable's work, and to what extent they may be expected to distort his style. The *Mill near Brighton* was one of the earliest plates to be undertaken by David Lucas – the first proofs bear the date 1829 – though in the end Constable rejected it for the parts of ENGLISH LANDSCAPE SCENERY published in his lifetime, and the final version was not produced for sale till the year after his death. There is no reason to suppose that this delay was due to any dissatisfaction on Constable's side with the quality of the print, which is indeed one of the most successful translations of a rough sketch into the black-and-white medium; more probably it is to be attributed to the subject-matter, which did not to his mind contrast sufficiently with the other themes he had chosen for the separate parts of his publication.

The original sketch, in the Victoria and Albert Museum, has a dark, broken, stormy sky; this goes to show that it was probably produced specifically for the engraving, around 1829, and certainly the mezzotint does not, and could not, enhance the tempestuous impression of the painting. But the shape of the clouds between the uppermost sails of the mill, and to their left, is altered in the print, and three birds have been added in the sky. The drawing of the nearer cottage has been made more precise in the mezzotint, and what is an indistinct fleck of colour in the sketch has become a figure walking along a path; the direction in which the figure is looking was altered during the process of engraving. In the oil sketch the foliage on the right goes almost to the top of the design; when Lucas began the mezzotint he copied it exactly, but Constable altered this during the proof stages, making the tree lower and more bushy in shape. In the print the weather vane is more conspicuous, and the drawing of the sails more detailed. It can be imagined how a copyist setting out to paint a 'Constable' from the mezzotint will imitate these changes in the drawing and the detail at one remove. A particular pitfall for the copyist of this subject is the shadow cast by the middle sail upon the side of the mill; although in Constable's original the difference between shadow and substance is clear enough, the copyist with only the print to work from almost invariably makes this dark area look nonsensically like a fourth sail.

A Summerland underwent a more radical change of mood in its translation to mezzotint. In this case Lucas was given an original painted fifteen or sixteen years before, in 1814, at the seminal period of Constable's communion with the scenery of the Stour Valley. The mood of the sketch, now in the Paul Mellon Collection, is, though cold, idyllic; it has a soft and summery sky darkened only on the left by a grey film of a passing shower. This was too serene to be passed without alteration by Constable in 1830. In the first proofs he had added to the sky a rainbow – a symbol which came to take more and more possession of his mind. This he removed before the published state was reached, replacing it by thin pencils of light throughout the upper air; contrast between light and dark in the whole composition is much emphasized, and the effect is sharper and stormier.

Similar changes took place between the sketch for *Spring, East Bergholt Common*, which was probably painted about the same time as *A Summerland*, and the mezzotint, which was one of the first four to be chosen for publication. The sky was in any event of more uncertain mien even in the sketch, the weather being described by Constable as 'Hail Squalls'; but in the print the effect of precipitation is made clearer, and the drawing of mill, horses, and ploughman is more detailed. In the same way the detail of the path in the left foreground is made more precise, stones are added in the right foreground, and the church steeple in the distance is sharpened in drawing.

Changes of a different nature took place between the oil sketch *Summer morning: Dedham from Langham* and the mezzotint which was issued in 1831. The definitive concept of this subject, a seminal one for Constable, was reached by him in 1812, the date of an oil sketch in the Ashmolean and a drawing at Copenhagen. He reverted to it on more than one page of his sketch-book of 1813, and in a sketch in the Tate Gallery; but it seems likely on stylistic grounds that he made a fresh oil sketch for the engraver when he was contemplating the introduction of the scene in ENGLISH LANDSCAPE SCENERY, combining in this version the landscape construction of his earlier paintings and drawings, but giving it a manifestly serene summer sky to accord with the mood of the title, and providing for the foreground an Arcadian shepherd boy playing the flute to a cow. The earlier proofs followed the sketch closely, but then Constable felt dissatisfied with these figures in the foreground. By progressive alterations on the engraver's plate they became, as in the published version, a milkmaid with a pail in place of the piping shepherd, two cows instead of one, and a plough in the left foreground. Through all these changes he left the untroubled calm of the high, almost cloudless sky undisturbed.

Since in planning ENGLISH LANDSCAPE SCENERY Constable was, at the age of fifty-three, reviewing his entire life's work, his choice of subject-matter is a revealing indication of the bent of his interests. A description of the bias of his choice is complex, since he caused a number of plates to be started and brought to publication pitch, and then decided not to use them. This was because he wanted to preserve within each part of four plates, and in the work as a whole, a proper balance of subjects and contrast of effects. Accordingly some thirty plates were called into being, of which twenty were used in the five parts published in his lifetime; the others saw the light of day in posthumous editions of 1838 and later years. Of the full range of subjects one-half were of scenes at Dedham, East Bergholt, Flatford, and the artist's homeland. They are headed by the view of his birthplace which he chose as the vignette for the title-page of the book, and include Willy Lott's House, Dedham Mill, and Dedham Vale. The remaining scenes are taken fairly uniformly from the other regions of his affection; three from Hampstead, two each from Brighton and Salisbury, individual plates from Helmingham, Weymouth, and Yarmouth. But more important in this context than the landscape represented was the weather effect reproduced in the plate. It was characteristic that the first two plates Constable ever asked Lucas to make before embarking on his opus were from water-colours of the Thames, entitled *Approaching Storm* and *Departing Storm*. Views of the fields near East Bergholt bore as their chief title *Summer Evening*, *Spring*, *A Summerland*, *Autumnal Sunset*, and *Summer Morning*; these names show at once how Constable's main preoccupation was with the cloudscape and the light, features which he included in the term the 'chiaroscuro of Nature' which the mezzotints were designed to embody.

In the midst of this absorbing business Constable found other occupations. His election as a full Academician led to his serving on the Hanging Committee for the 1830 Exhibition, an occasion when he had the mortification of seeing his own *Water-meadows near Salisbury*, which had been mis-sorted, rejected by the selectors as a 'nasty, green thing'. The following year he began teaching in the Life school, making the task more agreeable to himself by setting his figure of Eve amidst a bower of green boughs.

During these years his friendship with Leslie grew apace, encouraged by their joint interest in the practical concerns of the Academy. Their correspondence now much preponderates over the letters which were somewhat dilatorily exchanged between Constable and Fisher, who was beginning to ail. John Fisher's sudden death in 1832 broke the last link between the happier years of his rising fame and the embittered achievement of his ambition.

Constable had paid his last visits to Salisbury in 1829, beginning with a stay in July and returning for part of October and November. He worked prolifically, and in the oil sketches of the environs of Fisher's house in July had recaptured the former serenity of his style. It was on these visits that he conceived and set to work upon his last large-scale embodiment of the scene, his *Salisbury Cathedral from the Meadows*. Fisher referred to it on its inception as the 'Church under a cloud', with a side reference to the perils of the Establishment during the rising clamour for reform. Eventually it was forward enough to be shown at the Royal Academy in 1831. The painting is of approximately the same width as his canal scenes, but some 6 in. higher, to give greater prominence to the sky. The large sketch for it, in the Guildhall, suffered a strange fate in the late nineteenth century, when the Cathedral was concealed by a castle painted over it; this embellishment was not removed till the picture was cleaned in 1951. Once again Constable rifled Thomson's 'Summer' for a suitable quotation, choosing his description of the rainbow following storm clouds:

> As from the face of heaven the scatter'd clouds
> Tumultuous rove, th'interminable sky
> Sublimer swells, and o'er the world expands
> A purer azure through the lightened air
> A brighter lustre and a clearer calm
> Diffusive tremble; while as if in sign
> Of danger past, a glittering note of joy
> Set off abundant by the yellow sky
> Invests the fields, and nature smiles revived.

The painting embodies the artist's growing reverence for the rainbow as a symbol, so much so that his own name for this picture was 'The Rainbow'.

He was more than ever self-critical of the painting when it was returned unsold to his studio after the exhibition, and repainted it extensively in 1833 and 1834. This possibly explains why there is something unsatisfactory about the predominance of his later mannerism in the work as it now stands. It is a picture in which may well be seen some interaction between his current experiences with mezzotint and his practice as a painter on a grand scale. Lucas made a mezzotint from the exhibited picture, on a large plate which was approaching completion when Constable died; he also made a similar small plate from one of the preliminary sketches for the final version. It is interesting to see that the smaller plate was begun with no rainbow, but that a double rainbow was introduced during the proofing. In the extensive correspondence which he had with the engraver during the last weeks of his life Constable showed constant anxiety for the sky and particularly the rainbow, and the Victoria and Albert Museum has a proof touched with white to make this broader and more conspicuous.

In the following year, 1832, he felt that his *Waterloo Bridge from Whitehall Stairs* was at last ready for exhibition. No painting of his had a longer period of gestation. It represents the opening of Rennie's Waterloo Bridge with great pomp and circumstance by the Prince Regent on 18 June 1817. As the date was the second anniversary of the battle of Waterloo there was ample reason for general festivity and the presence of regiments which had fought in the battle; on the water were two Royal barges and the Lord Mayor's barge. No doubt Constable saw the scene, which was sufficiently imprinted on his memory to make him persevere through many discouragements to the conclusion of the work. He seems first to have conceived the project of painting the event two years later, in 1819, when he showed Farington a sketch to which he objected as too much of a 'bird's eye view'. Accordingly he began planning it at the time when he was embarking on his series of six-foot canal scenes, and probably in the very year when he had known the success of *The White Horse*. It was to be a metropolitan counterpart to the country river, full of pageantry of urban life at its most colourful and exciting. But the difference of content and feeling led to its postponement year after year. He thought of finishing it for the 1821 exhibition, but Farington recommended a work more like the *Stratford Mill* he had shown in the previous year. Constable was again quite determined to send the composition to the 1824 exhibition, but *The Lock* went instead, and in July he wrote to Fisher: 'I have no inclination to pursue my Waterloo; I am impressed with an idea that it will ruin me.' However, he got the outline on a new canvas in 1825, and proposed to complete it for the 1826 exhibition, to which he sent *The Cornfield* instead. The following year he added 2 ft to the left of the canvas, in order to include the terrace of Pembroke House and the elevation of Fife House as a more significant vertical conclusion to this side. Once again his engagement with mezzotinting acted as the catalyst and released the energy in him to finish the project. First proposed to Lucas in 1829, among his earliest subjects, he began engraving the plate in 1831. The opening of another Thames bridge, the new London Bridge, was no doubt another stimulus to activity. It is hardly surprising that even now the painting was, in the eyes both of Constable and of his friends, seriously unfinished when he eventually sent it to the exhibition of 1832. A reduction in the number of varnishing days deprived him of some of the time he felt he needed to pull it together. But the reduced number of days did not pass without incident. *Waterloo Bridge* is unusual among Constable's pictures in the amount of red it contains. A cool grey picture by Turner was hung next to it. In the time left for final adjustments Turner put a small red seal on his own painting, working it into the shape of a buoy and making Constable's colours weaker in effect. 'He has been here,' said Constable, 'and fired a gun.' Once more the artist worked on his picture after the exhibition; and he was still brushing it up in 1834, fortunately without destroying the effect.

He attributed the failure of this painting to attract attention partly to the absence of his redeeming voice, 'The Rural'; certainly it was the absence of that voice which had made the path to its completion so long and so uncertain. On the built-up banks of the Thames he had no store of visual memories and childhood associations to fall back on, as he had for the Stour. Hence there exist an unusual number of *ad hoc* studies of the river looking towards Waterloo Bridge, made during the tortuous progress of the plan, as well as others which show him designing the treatment of the ceremonial adjuncts. As far as possible he concentrated on the great sweep of sky and the sparkle of the river water, but the subject impelled him to pay close attention to the hard facts of bricks and mortar, the riverside houses and wharves, the bridge itself, as well as the beflagged barges and gaily clad soldiers.

Besides these studies there are two full-scale versions of the subject. That belonging to Lord Fairhaven is probably the earlier; measuring 8 ft by 5 ft, it is overall the largest of all Constable's pictures, and the width suggests that it is the actual canvas to which he added 2 ft after his visit in 1827 to Pembroke House. The exhibited version is slightly smaller, yet includes more of the house in the left foreground. Evidently Constable copied the outline of Lord Fairhaven's picture on to a new canvas for the version he finally showed, making some alterations in detail and general effect. Its surface is a finely vibrant one, and it is said that Peter de Wint, the water-colour painter, admired it so much that he offered Constable a silver palette knife in place of the one he had used on it.

Although in 1834 and 1835 Constable turned to earlier sketches made in Wiltshire for large water-colours of Old Sarum and Stonehenge, he had virtually taken his leave of Salisbury in the grand manner when he showed *Salisbury Cathedral from the Meadows* in 1831. The completion of *Waterloo Bridge from Whitehall Stairs* in the following year concluded his one ambitious composition on a theme

from the centre of London, where he had lived on and off
for over thirty years. Now he showed an unusual readiness
for change, and for savouring the experience of different
places. Thus in 1831 he visited Digby Neave at Pitt Place,
Epsom, where he made a drawing of the house in which
Lord Lyttelton died after seeing a ghost. He also sketched
the local type of plough, known as Double Tom. In 1832
he visited Englefield House in Berkshire, as a result of a
commission to paint the seat from the owner, Mr Benyon
de Beauvoir. The outcome was perhaps not entirely satis-
factory, but it illustrates interestingly enough the difference
between Constable's concept of landscape painting and the
older topographical viewpoint which was by no means
dead in his patron's mind. Mr Benyon de Beauvoir objected
to cows being placed in the foreground, saying that it
'looked as if he had his farmyard before his drawing-room
windows'. Constable duly replaced the offending stock by
deer, but he can hardly have relished being compared un-
favourably with one Milbourne, a sort of sub-Zuccarelli
painter who had made an earlier view of the house. When
it was sent to the Academy in 1833 the President, Shee, said
that it ought to be in the Architectural Room, since it was
only a picture of a house. To this Constable replied with
his usual spirit that it was 'a picture of a summer morning including a house'. But, though he had said during its
execution 'My house tires me very much. The windows and
window frames, and chimneys and chimney pots are end-
less', he was refreshed by the genuine and rightly directed
admiration of Lady Morley. She said to him: 'How fresh,
how dewy, how exhilarating', and he replied that 'half of
this, if I could think I deserved it, was worth all the talk
and cant about pictures in the world'. During his visit to
Englefield House he paid a visit to Stoke Poges which gave
him ideas for some illustrations to an edition of Gray's
Elegy produced in 1834.

Late in 1833 he went to Folkestone, where his eldest son,
John, was at school; a number of water-colour sketches
he made on this visit are in the British Museum. A more
fundamental impact on his mind was made by the exten-

sive knowledge of Sussex scenery he acquired in 1834 and 1835. This came about through his friendship with a namesake, George Constable, who lived at Arundel. George Constable, who was no relation, was an amateur artist of some ability, and was a perceptive judge of his friend's work. So perceptive, in fact, that he became one of the earliest utterers of faked Constables; having borrowed some oil sketches, he made copies of them and for some unfathomable reason sold them as originals after the painter's death. But no shadow of this deception troubled John Constable during his lifetime; and he not only found his friend a congenial host but delighted in the countryside around Arundel. Almost for the first time he found himself in sympathy with a rolling countryside dominated by wooded slopes; in fact, the conventionally beautiful. As he himself wrote to Leslie in the full tide of his enthusiasm, 'the woods hang from excessive steeps and precipices and the trees are beyond everything beautiful; I never saw such beauty in natural landscape before. I wish it may influence what I do in future, for I have too much preferred the picturesque to the beautiful, which will I hope account for the broken ruggedness of my style.'

In consequence he went on a crowded programme of visits to Chichester, Fittleworth, and Petworth as well as to the surroundings of Arundel and its Castle. He returned to Petworth for a fortnight in September, as the guest of Lord Egremont; since he did not feel particularly at ease in grand company, he arranged to accept this invitation when Leslie could also be there. Lord Egremont was at this time 83 years old, but still active and attentive to the guests with whom he delighted to surround himself. Even the cantankerous Haydon could find nothing but good to record of this truly benevolent man and wrote: 'The very animals at Petworth seemed happier than in any other spot on Earth – better fed, and their dumbness and helpless dependence on Man more humanely felt for. He was one of those left of the old School who considered a great Artist as fit society for any Men, however high their station or eminent their rank.'

On these two visits, and a further visit to Arundel of just over a fortnight in 1835, Constable engaged in a spate of sketching, as though he were nervous of losing any nuance of the scenes which were charming him by their novelty. By far the greater number of his sketches of these two years are in the Victoria and Albert Museum; they include a complete sketch-book used in 1835. Another large group, including most of those he made at Cowdray, which he visited from Petworth in 1834, is in the British Museum. It is possible to form from them a complete impression of his latest style as a draughtsman. A prominent feature is the use of water-colour to a degree not apparent earlier in his sketches from Nature. He washes his drawings with a lightness of tone and subtlety of colour which puts him among the most sensitive users of the medium. His pencil drawings are far more dynamic than before, completed without the tightness and hardness which sometimes gives an impression of laboured thought to earlier productions. This freer style reaches its extreme in an exciting calligraphic shorthand. But he seems to have made no oil sketches on these visits.

Another sign of change in Constable's temperament was the comparative speed with which he digested the experience of a new environment sufficiently to make a large composition out of it. His *Arundel Mill and Castle* was planned for the Academy exhibition of 1836, and though postponed in favour of *The Cenotaph* was settled on for his exhibit in 1837. He worked on it the day before he died, and the painting was considered by his friends sufficiently finished to be shown as a memorial of him. It is not on his largest scale, measuring only 40 × 29 in., but it is a fully thought-out and carefully conceived embodiment of his feelings for the castle-crowned crag. In the foreground, the Mill, on a site used for this purpose since the Domesday Book, both links the subject to Constable's perpetual tastes for riverside industry and provides the sense of historic continuity he had so much valued on the Stour. The composition follows with considerable accuracy the drawing he made on the spot during his last visit, but he has added in the foreground his favourite theme of two boys fishing. Over it all he has cast the flickering patina of his latest manner, preserved in all the greater purity because he did not live to finish the picture for exhibition or to work on it after return to his studio.

While he was making contact with new places Constable did not neglect Suffolk, and the warm family feeling between him and his brother Abram was enhanced by their common interest in the future of Constable's motherless children. But he did not now sketch so frequently and assiduously amongst the familiar scenes. An exception was provided by his summer visit of 1832, when he took his eldest daughter, Maria ('Minna') down to Dedham at the end of July to recuperate from a serious attack of scarlet fever. Later the same year he had the melancholy duty of attending the funeral of his young assistant, John Dunthorne, who had died in November. On these two visits he made a number of sketches of cottages at East Bergholt. These are in an unusual technique of water-colour with a bistre pen outline. In subject-matter they revert to his interests of thirty-five years before, when he was sending his sketches of picturesque cottages to J. T. Smith in the hope that some might be worthy of etching.

The last visible affirmation of his feeling for his homeland was revealed in the painting *The Valley Farm* which he exhibited at the Academy in 1835. This is a view of Willy Lott's house, the building which figures in *The Hay Wain*, seen from the other bank of the branch of the river nearest the house. It will be recalled that this farmhouse appealed to Constable's deepest sense of continuity. If this is the painting referred to in a letter of September 1834 to Leslie, 'I have almost determined to attack another canal for my large frame', it was a deliberate return to the subjects, if not the handling and mood, of ten years before – a successor to the six great Stour scenes. The action of the piece resides in the ferry boat (seen also in the painting at Ipswich, *The Mill Stream*), in which a young lady with her shopping-basket is being poled across to the bank near Dedham.

If in painting the picture Constable was returning to the series he had abandoned ten years before, he went even farther back for the sketches and models used in the work. The first certain hints of it – indeed the only dated fore-runners – are two small drawings in the sketch-book of 1813. He also tackled the subject twice before painting the picture which is now in the Tate Gallery. One of these is nearly the same size as the final version, but appears to have been painted at about the same time as the pencil sketch. The other, one-quarter the size, seems from its style to have been painted in the 1820s. In addition there are two small-scale compositional oil sketches in the Victoria and Albert Museum which look as though they were made to settle the details of the last version. An unusual feature of the preliminary work is the sketch of a Suffolk child which Constable used in reverse for the figure of the woman seated in the boat.

This variety of preparatory work of all periods which precedes *The Valley Farm* indicates the great importance the subject had for Constable. Most puzzling is the relation-ship to the final work of the two large drawings of ash trees in the Victoria and Albert Museum. One was en-larged from a drawing from Nature perhaps seventeen years before; the same tree, with additions to its crown, occurs in the right foreground of *The Valley Farm*. Its companion is copied with variations from the tree in the left foreground of *Salisbury Cathedral from the Meadows*, and must have been drawn later than the painting, since it is on paper watermarked 1833. He seems to have made the drawings to show at his lecture at Hampstead in 1836, and he refers to the second as a young lady who died of a broken heart because she had a board labelled 'All vagrants and beggars will be dealt with according to law' nailed to her side.

For *The Valley Farm* Constable embellished the farm-house, giving a greater air of consequence to the windows. He had the uncommon experience of selling the picture from his easel before sending it to the exhibition. The purchaser was Robert Vernon, one of the rising collectors who, like John Sheepshanks, was beginning to form a gallery of modern British painting. Following his usual custom, Constable took the painting back from the Academy to work on further, keeping it from the impatient owner till its return from further exhibition at the British Institution in January 1836. He described his final touches to John Chalon: 'Oiling out, making out, polishing, scraping, etc., seem to have agreed with it exceedingly. The "sleet" and "snow" have disappeared, leaving in their places, silver, ivory, and a little gold.' It is a tempting description, reminiscent of the advice West had given the young painter more than thirty years before: 'Your darks should look like the darks of silver, not of lead or of slate.' But unfortunately, the final condition of the painting does not bear out Constable's enthusiasm. His inability to let well alone, and the tendency to fidget which increased with his more deliberate works in his later years, have upset the fine balance which generally subsists between his content and his execution. The painting gives the impression that the artist has for once lost his normal feeling of immediate contact with his subject. Possibly the comparative rarity of his visits to Suffolk of late years helps to explain this defect.

If, when Constable wrote to Leslie in September 1834 'I have almost determined to attack another canal for my large frame', he was not referring to *The Valley Farm*, he may have had in mind an interlinked horizontal composition which is known in a number of preparatory sketches and possibly unfinished pictures, and is perhaps best called *A Farmhouse on the River's Edge*. Thus there are a drawing of 1829 in a private collection, a water-colour in the British Museum, a small oil sketch in the Victoria and Albert Museum and larger, later paintings in the Phillips Collection, Washington, and the Kennedy Memorial Gallery in Los Angeles. It seems possible that the farmhouse started off as a representation of Willy Lott's house, but was changed out of recognition during the progress of the work; certainly one of these compositions has been traditionally called 'The Valley Farm'. The theme of a boat on the water, similar to the ferry in the Tate Gallery's picture, is common to all. If Constable had attempted a six-foot canvas of this horizontal subject he would have made of it something more in keeping with *The Hay Wain* and *The Leaping Horse* than *The Valley Farm* in fact became; it is one of those open umbrageous riverside scenes which reflect the quintessence of his most successful compositions. As it is, the whole group of studies embodies the finest characteristics of the last phase of his art.

For in the final years of his life Constable's style did develop, and in a more creative way than would be judged from the rather exaggerated 'manner' of *Salisbury Cathedral from the Meadows* and *The Valley Farm*. This latest development is at its most brilliant in the horizontal compositions just discussed. There is a new lightness in his conception of the scene, and the harmony of colours is softer and more conceptual than perceived. Thus in *The Farmhouse near the Water's Edge* in the Victoria and Albert Museum, the scheme ranges from the pinkish-brown of the farmhouse roof to the dark blue-green of the shadows under the trees. Much of the middle tint of the trees is in an unnaturalistic yellowish green, and a flickering rhythm is given to the whole by the little accents of reflected light. This last phase of his painting technique suggests that he may have been working his way towards an abstraction from his normal style which, if in no sense like Turner's last great visions of colour, might have been equally different from his earlier manner. In all the Constable canon it is the least well known of his variations, and is a style which may owe something to the greater use he made of water-colour in the last eight years of his life.

For this increasing use of water-colour is another noticeable change. After his visit to the Lake District in 1806 he had rarely washed his drawings, and when he did so it was mainly in monochrome greys. Latterly he may have come to feel a disinclination to encumber himself with the fuller equipment of oil sketching when working in the open air; but there seems equally to have been a genuine shift in his interest to the lighter and more evanescent tones of the water medium, long established in the English school. The change of emphasis becomes fully apparent in the sketch-book of drawings, in ink outline washed with delicate colour, he used at East Bergholt in 1832. It became more certainly established when, because of a long illness in the winter of 1833 and spring of 1834, he could send only drawings to the Academy; these included his large water-colour *Old Sarum* which was at that time his largest, most ambitious, and most carefully worked-up exercise in the medium. For this composition he chose a subject which appealed to his sense of history – 'a city turned into a land-scape, independently of the historical associations with old Sarum, could not but be interesting to Constable,' says Leslie – and he took up a work of which he had painted an oil sketch for Lucas to engrave, enlarging it in size, giving it a more varied chiaroscuro, and introducing the rainbow which haunted him as a symbol.

The success of this work he followed with larger and subtler open-air sketches in water-colour on his visits to Arundel and Petworth during the summer and autumn of 1834. Some of the drawings he made at this time, such as *Petworth House from the Park*, rival any contemporary water-colours by their skilful use of the medium. When in London he used the same devices to produce misty evocations of the Thames Valley dominated by the dome of St Paul's as seen from his house in Well Walk, Hamp-stead. Even more extreme in their expressionism and masterly in their concentration are the few brilliant mono-chromes in pencil and sepia wash he made in the last few years of his life. Full of energy and reminiscent of Claude's drawings, these are the most spare and concise summing up of his vision of the Stour.

With this greater interest in water-colour and wash draw-ing went a diminution of oil sketching. Constable's last concentrated period of productivity seems to have occurred around the years 1829 and 1830, comprising the open-air sketches he made on his last visits to John Fisher and con-tinuing with the studies he worked up in his studio for engraving by David Lucas. Some seem topographically associated with his Sussex visits; others revert to the Stour. Like the sketches for the *Farmhouse near the Water's Edge*, these late works show a continually more advanced ductility of handling. Here again we can see the effect that working in water-colour has had on his use of oil, and the assurance created by his life's experience is to be felt in the energy of his interpretation. It is a paradox of development that Turner should have carried over the essentials of his early water-colour technique into his finest oils, while Constable shows the effect of the more fluid medium in his very latest work alone. In such works (and this is true of *Stoke-by-Nayland*, *A Cottage at East Bergholt* and *Arundel Mill and Castle* on a larger scale), his effort to catch a transitory effect results in an even more transitory impression on the canvas; no longer does he study to represent slowly moving shadows cast by the midday sun, but the briefest flicker of flowing water or the impermanent light cast by fast-moving clouds.

CONCLUSION

CONSTABLE had inherited a good deal of the business sense of his mill-owning forebears, and though he had abandoned commerce to become a professional painter few people could have conformed less to the conventional idea of the feckless, Bohemian artist. He regarded both his pictures and the money he inherited as property held in trust for his children. This trait was apparent as early as 1821, when he commented that his painting *Trees near Hampstead Church* might one day fetch as much for his children as if he had bought the field in which they grew – a surprisingly shrewd assessment of their relative present-day values. This sense lay at the bottom of his self-reproaches for having squandered money on publishing ENGLISH LANDSCAPE SCENERY.

But that publication had crystallized another aspect of his thought which developed in the last years of his life – that is, his desire to act as a propagandist for the art of landscape painting. As has been seen, canvassing to become a full R.A. had been made an agony for him through the tendency of the members to explain to him the inferior place landscape held in opposition to high art. At the time he held his tongue, so as not to prejudice his election, but when it was all over he set to work to justify his estimate of landscape painting, first in the text for ENGLISH LANDSCAPE SCENERY, and then in the lectures which he delivered between 1833 and 1836. These were not simply compilations from existing sources, but the products of his own acute analysis and original research. It would be difficult to name any earlier survey of the subject to rival in depth and understanding the four lectures on the History of Landscape Painting which he delivered at the Royal Institution in May and June 1836, of which Leslie gives a transcript. These sum up all his reflections on the subject and his conversations with his friends. As is inevitable when a painter talks about other painters, the lectures are full of prejudices – Both, Berchem, Boucher, David, come in for particularly heavy condemnation – but against this can be set the speaker's eloquent enthusiasm for Claude, Ruisdael, Gainsborough, Wilson, and Cozens. The management of these lectures shows, as much as the arresting phrases of his correspondence and reported conversation, the lively culture of his mind. His unusual powers of self-expression make him one of the most quotable of painters. He gives penetrating descriptions of the paintings he most admires. Of Rembrandt's 'Mill' (now in the National Gallery of Art, Washington) he said: 'This is the first picture in which a sentiment has been expressed by the chiaroscuro only, all details being excluded.' Of Titian's 'St Peter Martyr' he gave a notably perceptive account, which he illustrated with a large-scale copy of alternative sketches for the fallen figure of the saint. Here he says, taking an image from music, of which he was an adept: 'It is striking to observe with what consummate skill the painter, like a great musician, has varied his touch and execution from slow movements to those of extreme rapidity. Thus the quick and vivid sparks of light near and upon the assassin's arm, hand and sword give inconceivable energy to his action and contrast finely with the solemn quiet of the retiring forest.'

Although not a Bohemian, Constable had his fair share of temperament and was quite capable of behaving intolerably when things were going badly for him or when he was oppressed by ill health or anxiety. This alternation in his behaviour helps to account for the varying estimates that were formed of his character. His closest friends admired him greatly for his personal qualities; to take a little-known example, Trimmer, who had been a pupil of Turner's, described him as 'by far the most agreeable artist I ever knew'. On the other hand, it is hardly surprising that, for instance, Linnell or Collins, about whom Constable had spread scandalous gossip, were less enthusiastic. Richard Redgrave, who had suffered under his tongue as a pupil, recorded in his MEMOIR that, in Leslie's LIFE, Constable 'appears all amiability and goodness, and one cannot recognize the bland, yet intense, sarcasm of his nature: soft and amiable in speech, he yet uttered sarcasms which cut you to the bone.'

Those who knew him personally emphasize his passionate love of children; above all, of course, his own. A pleasant illustration of this trait, attested by a great number of statements and anecdotes, is the tale of Charles Mayne Young's visit to Constable to see a painting on which he was working. When they reached the studio they found it badly torn by a broom handle. All Constable had to say to the boy who had done it was: 'Oh! my dear pet! See what we have done! Dear, dear! What shall we do to mend it? I can't think – can *you*?'

We have seen how the use of water-colour became a prominent feature of his work in the 1830s, and the extent to which he had begun to think in the terms of this medium is apparent even in *The Cenotaph*, which was the large oil he exhibited at the Royal Academy in 1836. There is a lightness and a flicker of accents about it more in keeping with the water-colour *Stonehenge* he showed at the same time than with his earlier oil-paintings. The work displays a new colour harmony, and the sky has a curious transparency which is almost flimsiness, constant with its being an autumnal subject. Constable laid aside the *Arundel Mill and Castle* on which he was working to complete this picture for the 1836 exhibition. In deciding to do so he was guided by the circumstance that the Academy was showing for the last time in its first home, Somerset House, before moving to its new accommodation in a wing of the present National Gallery. 'I preferred to see Sir Joshua Reynolds' name and Sir George Beaumont's once more in the catalogue for the last time at the old house,' he wrote. He based the painting on the drawing he had made at Coleorton in 1823 of the cenotaph which Beaumont erected in his grounds to Reynolds's memory, and on which he had inscribed Wordsworth's lines. The coincidence by which this became Constable's last exhibit during his lifetime has often been commented upon, as has the fact that he was the last visitor to the Life School at Somerset House. Redgrave wrote of this visit: 'Poor Constable! He left Somerset House that night only to die. Yet on that occasion he was, as usual, full of jokes and gibes, and he indulged in the vein of satire he was ever so fond of.'

Death when it came was mercifully sudden. On the last day of March 1837 he had worked at *Arundel Mill and Castle*, which was almost due for the exhibition. That evening he went out to perform an act of kindness. Shortly after going to sleep he woke in great pain, and within an hour he was dead.

There was no immediately spectacular increase in his repute, and the growth of his fame to its present pitch was reached only by slow and gradual stages. A body of subscribers headed by Beechey gave *The Cornfield* to the National Gallery in the year of his death, preferring it, in the circumstances related, to *Salisbury Cathedral from the Meadows*. Since there were at that time only 130 paintings in the collection and the English School, apart from Hogarth and Reynolds, was only scantily represented amongst them, this was indeed an act of courage and a declaration that he was fit for the Pantheon. The next year, however, the sale of the contents of his studio brought in very little, and much of the important material was bought in on his family's behalf.

Paradoxically, the most encouraging evidence of interest in Constable's style lay in the appearance of forgeries soon after his death. Some of them were the imitations of his sketches sold by his Arundel friend George Constable, and unmasked by Leslie. None the less a genuine enthusiasm was arising: for instance, Edward Fitzgerald, the author of OMAR KHAYYAM, bought a large picture in 1841 and wrote that it had 'a dash and felicity in the execution which gives one a thrill of good digestion in one's room, and the thought of which makes one inclined to jump over the children's heads in the streets'.

Devotees of Turner are rarely entirely at ease with Constable, and Ruskin took the lead in expressing his sense of the deficiencies of an art he might have been expected to admire for its truth to nature. All he could say was that this painter's mind was vulgar, and that he 'perceives in a landscape that the grass is wet, the meadows flat and the boughs shady; that is to say, about as much, I suppose, might in general be apprehended, between them, by an intelligent fawn and a sky-lark'. But the steady growth of his fame in England went on. Leslie's enthusiasm, embodied in his remarkably detailed and well-organized MEMOIRS OF THE LIFE OF JOHN CONSTABLE, first published in 1843, helped to spread knowledge and understanding of his friend's work. Ultimately, Miss Isabel Constable's gift, in 1888, to the Victoria and Albert Museum of nearly 100 paintings and 300 drawings brought the brilliance of his oil sketches into prominence at a time when public taste was ready to receive them.

In France his repute which, as we have seen, was a real influence on the landscape painters of the 1820s, to some extent went underground. Even so, Constant Troyon had made a point of seeing the full-scale sketches of *The Hay Wain* and *The Leaping Horse* when they were with the dealer D. T. White in 1853, and much wanted to buy them. When, however, the Impressionists emerged as young revolutionaries, sweeping out-moded conventions on one side, the effect of the English painter on their own mentors had been forgotten.

The precise naturalism of Constable's art calls to mind Nathaniel Hawthorne's description of Anthony Trollope's novels: 'just as real as if some giant had hewn a great lump out of the earth, and put it under a glass case, with all its inhabitants going about their daily business, and not suspecting that they were made a show of'. The strict limitations Constable imposed upon his travels and subjects might seem to represent the parochial and insular mentality to be expected of an Englishman. But the exactly contemporary example of Turner, who took the whole practicable world as his subject, would be sufficient – even if there were not many others, for instance, Wilson, Towne, Cozens – to show that this was no national trait, but the reflex of Constable's own personal need. It made him, in Leslie's phrase, 'the most genuine painter of English landscape'. His ultimate triumph was as much an achievement of character as of genius. He felt his isolation, and the lack of fashionable understanding, and although it warped his judgement of people it did not deflect the integrity of his purpose. Outwardly his life was a tempestuous battle, but the world he entered in his painting-room was a secluded garden, and no one has more completely communicated the euphoria of the English countryside.

SELECT BIBLIOGRAPHY

The following list includes only monographs which contain significant new or original material on John Constable.

C. R. LESLIE. *Memoirs of the Life of John Constable, R.A.* 1843.

First published six years after the artist's death, with mezzotints by David Lucas, this remarkable work was written with affectionate understanding of its subject, based upon a long friendship. Leslie supplemented his personal knowledge with painstaking research, and his work remains an essential introduction to the full knowledge of Constable. It remains one of the most enduringly interesting of biographies, and its continuing appeal is proved by the number of new editions which have been called for.

A second edition with new material was published in 1845, and a third, with an introduction by the editor's son, R. C. Leslie, in 1896. It was republished in Everyman's Library, with an introduction by Sir Charles J. Holmes, in 1912. A fuller, re-edited edition, with a substantial corpus of plates and additions to the text of the letters was produced for the centenary year, 1937, by the Hon. Andrew Shirley.

The most recent editions are by Benedict Nicolson for the Chiltern Library, 1949, and, with numerous illustrations, by J. H. Mayne for the Phaidon Press, 1951.

The French translation of 1905 contains a valuable introductory essay by L. Bazalgette, 'Constable et les Paysagistes de 1830'. A Russian translation by A. D. Chegodaev appeared in 1964.

SIR CHARLES J. HOLMES. *Constable and his Influence on Landscape Painting.* 1902.

This was the first full-length critical account of Constable's work to be published. The author had a discerning eye and a keen sense for the chronological development of Constable's work which ensure that his lists, though not entirely free from the faults to be expected in all pioneering work, are still basically reliable.

LORD WINDSOR. *John Constable R.A.* 1903.

THE HON. ANDREW SHIRLEY. *The Published Mezzotints of David Lucas after John Constable, R.A.* 1930.
This gives the correspondence between Constable and Lucas. All the mezzotints are reproduced, and their states described.

PETER LESLIE. *Letters from John Constable, R.A. to C. R. Leslie, R.A.* 1931.

S. J. KEY. *John Constable: his Life and Work.* 1948.

G. REYNOLDS. *Catalogue of the Constable Collection in the Victoria and Albert Museum.* 1960.
This gives a full description and dating of the largest and most comprehensive individual collection of Constable's works. All the 597 component items are reproduced, on 310 black-and-white plates and one colour plate.

R. B. BECKETT. *John Constable and the Fishers. The Record of a Friendship.* 1952.
 John Constable's Correspondence. I. The Family at East Bergholt 1807–1837. 1962. *II. Early Friends and Maria Bicknell (Mrs Constable).* 1964. (further volumes in preparation)
The volumes so far published give rather more than half of a complete transcription of all the known letters from or to Constable, remarkable both in its thoroughness and in its accuracy. The text, which considerably augments Leslie and corrects him in some particulars, is linked by an explanatory account. The unpublished parts of the redaction are deposited for the use of students, in typescript, in the Library of the Victoria and Albert Museum. This series is indispensable to all students of Constable's life and work.

INDEX